Realism and Power

Postmodernism plays – seriously – with the structures of cultural authority. Focusing on the subversive techniques of British postmodernist fiction, Lee examines its challenge to Realist traditions, and the liberal humanist ideology behind it.

Lee provides a lively analysis of the ways in which postmodern British novels deliberately use Realist conventions and concepts and subvert them from within the very conventions they seek to transgress.

Exploring the concept of literary postmodernism, and the strategies and philosophies to which it has given rise, Lee investigates how they are developed in a selection of contemporary British novels, such as *Midnight's Children*, *Waterland*, *Flaubert's Parrot*, and *Lanark*. With refreshing directness, Lee looks at postmodernism in relation to history, the visual and performing arts, popular culture, including advertizing, music videos, and popular fiction, notably Stephen King's *Misery*.

Well argued and lucid, *Realism and Power* will be essential reading for students and teachers of literary and cultural studies.

Alison Lee is Assistant Professor of English at the University of Western Ontario, Canada.

Realism and Power
Postmodern British Fiction

Alison Lee

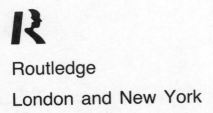

Routledge

London and New York

First published 1990
by Routledge
11 New Fetter Lane, London EC4P 4EE

Simultaneously published in the USA and Canada
by Routledge
a division of Routledge, Chapman and Hall, Inc.
29 West 35th Street, New York, NY 10001

© 1990 Alison Lee
Disc conversion by Columns Typesetters of Reading
Printed in Great Britain by Richard Clay Ltd, Bungay

British Library Cataloguing in Publication Data
Lee, Alison
    Realism and power: postmodern British fiction.
    1. Fiction in English 1945 — Postmodernism.
    Critical Studies
    I. Title
    823'.914 '09

PR
888
, P69
L4
1990

Library of Congress Cataloging in Publication Data
Lee, Alison, 1957–
    Realism and power: postmodern British fiction/Alison Lee.
    p.   cm.
    Bibliography: p.
    Includes index.
    1. English fiction — 20th century — History and criticism.
2. Postmodernism (Literature) — Great Britain. 3. Power (Social
sciences) in literature. 4. Realism in literature. I. Title.
PR888.P69L4   1989
823'.910912—dc20   89–10179
                    CIP

ISBN HB 0–415–04452–9
      PB 0–415–04103–1

Contents

Acknowledgements

I owe an enormous debt of thanks to Linda Hutcheon who first taught me about postmodernism. To a generation of graduate students at McMaster University, she has been an example of rigorous scholarship and professionalism, as well as a thought-provoking teacher and critic, and a generous friend.

My friend Leila Ryan not only provided me with a wonderful garret in which to complete my study, but has also been a careful reader and perceptive critic. Many other friends and colleagues have been remarkably good-humored about lengthy discussions on the topic and I am grateful to them for their help. Among these, Anthony Brennan, James King, Susan Bennett, Maria DiCenzo, Graham Knight, Barbara Brown, and Aruna Srivastava have provided both encouragement and insight. The Faculty of Arts at the University of Western Ontario gave me a generous grant to help with the final preparation of the manuscript, and Sue Desmond was a great help with the final typescript. The illustrations are from *Lanark* and are reproduced by kind permission of Alasdair Gray. Finally, my family have, as always, been supportive in ways far too numerous to mention.

The author and publishers would like to thank the following for permission to include in this volume passages from the sources indicated: Jonathan Cape Ltd (for Julian Barnes, *Flaubert's Parrot* and for Salman Rushdie, *Midnight's Children*), Faber & Faber Ltd (for Nigel Williams, *Star Turn*), Hamish Hamilton Ltd (for Peter Ackroyd, *Hawksmoor* © Peter Ackroyd 1984), William Heinemann Limited (for Graham Swift, *Waterland*, reprinted by permission of William Heinemann Limited), Anthony Sheil Associates Ltd (for Peter Ackroyd, *Hawksmoor*, © Peter

Ackroyd 1984, first published by Hamish Hamilton Ltd, London, and for John Fowles, *Daniel Martin*, © John Fowles, first published by Jonathan Cape Ltd, and John Fowles, *The Magus*, © John Fowles, first published by Jonathan Cape Ltd), A.P. Watt Ltd on behalf of Graham Swift (Graham Swift, *Waterland*). Permission has been requested from George Braziller, Inc., New York, to include passages from *Lanark* by Alasdair Gray.

Preface

Camel . . . did not seem to be particularly old, but he had been doing his Ph.D. thesis as long as anyone could remember. Its title – "Sanitation in Victorian Fiction" – seemed modest enough; but, as Camel would patiently explain, the absence of references to sanitation was as significant as the presence of the same, and his work thus embraced the entire corpus of Victorian fiction. Further, the Victorian period was best understood as a period of transition in which the comic treatment of human excretion in the eighteenth century was suppressed, or sublimated in terms of social reform, until it re-emerged as a source of literary symbolism in the work of Joyce and other moderns. Camel's preparatory reading spread out in wider and wider circles, and it often seemed that he was bent on exhausting the entire resources of the Museum library before commencing composition. Some time ago a wild rumour had swept through Bloomsbury to the effect that Camel had written his first chapter, on the hygiene of Neanderthal Man. . . .

David Lodge, *The British Museum is Falling Down*, 1983: 40

Writing about literary movements requires definitions, and trying to define Realism and postmodernism is a task which partakes of similarly wide circles, wild rumors, and ever-receding historical references to the ones Camel encounters above. For the purposes of this study, Realism, as I discuss in Chapter one, is limited to the literary conventions (and their ideological[1] implications) which were developed in nineteenth-century England and France as a formula for the literal transcription of "reality" into art. The debate over Realism is one which has existed since Plato and Aristotle, and Realism is, even now, a dominant frame of reference for literary criticism and evaluation. My focus in this study is on the challenge to literary Realism by postmodern techniques and conventions which seek to subvert the assumptions that Realism and its related ideology – what we usually call liberal humanism – have encouraged readers and teachers of literature to think of as "natural," "normal," and "neutral." Common sense and the transparency of language – as well as subjectivity, truth, meaning, and value – are terms and concepts which are still on the syllabus of the academy, and which postmodern novels try to question and draw attention to *as* conventions.

The term "postmodern" has had a troubled and hotly disputed beginning. However, despite the problems with the term itself – its relation to modernism, the meaning of "post," the periodization implied by the reference to modernism, and its co-opting of the modernism it apparently seeks to transgress – it has nevertheless entered the language, although what it designates is still very much at issue.[2] In the sense that I am using it throughout this study, postmodern is not a synonym for contemporary. Techniques that I discuss in relation to such novels as John Fowles' *The Magus* (1966, 1977b), Salman Rushdie's *Midnight's Children* (1981), or Peter Ackroyd's *Hawksmoor* (1985), are equally apparent in Miguel de Cervantes' *Don Quixote* (1604, 1614) or Laurence Sterne's *The Life and Opinions of Tristram Shandy* (1759–67). However, the frequency of such techniques in novels written since the 1960s has demanded that critical attention should be paid to them. Linda Hutcheon describes the postmodern as the "contradictory phenomenon that uses and abuses, installs and then subverts, the very concepts it challenges – be it in literature, painting, sculpture, film, video, dance, television, music, philosophy, aesthetic theory, psychoanalysis, linguistics or historiography" (1987: 10). Similarly, Jean-François Lyotard, in *The Postmodern Condition*, characterizes the postmodern as possessing an "incredulity toward metanarratives" (1984: xxiv), and Craig Owens, in "The Discourse of Others: Feminists and Postmodernism," calls it a "crisis of cultural authority, specifically of the authority vested in Western European culture and its institutions" (1985: 57). It is this subversive aspect of postmodern techniques that I have chosen as my focus and definition.

In questioning this "cultural authority," and its apparently eternal and transcendental truths, postmodernism shares concerns with those who, because of class, race, gender, or sexual preference, are "other" than, and have been marginalized by, the dominant tradition. Recent studies, such as Patricia Waugh's *Feminine Fictions*, have lamented the lack of critical attention paid to feminist postmodern writers who have been marginalized even within a fiction which concerns itself with questioning margins and boundaries valorized by the dominant cultural authority. The literary authors in this text are male, but it is not my purpose here to privilege one gender over another. One of postmodernism's most important concerns is to decenter the humanist notion of "individuality," of a coherent essence of self which exists outside ideology. Postmodern texts place the subject firmly within political, social, class, racial, and gender forces acting upon him/her. Linda Hutcheon points out in *A Poetics of Postmodernism* that the "assertion of identity through difference and specificity is a constant in postmodern thought" (1988: 59):

> Cultural homogenization too reveals its fissures, but the heterogeneity that is asserted in the face of that totalizing (yet pluralizing) culture does not take the form of many fixed individual subjects . . . but instead is conceived of as a flux of contextualized identities: contextualized by gender, class, race, ethnicity, sexual preference, education, social role and so on.
>
> (Hutcheon 1988: 59)

Studies in black, gay, native, and women's literature have taught us, indeed, that identity is produced in and by a system of differences. After all, as Waugh argues,

> for those marginalized by the dominant culture, a sense of identity as constructed through impersonal and social relations of power (rather than a sense of identity as the reflection of inner "essence") has been a major aspect of their self-concept long before post-structuralists and postmodernists began to assemble their cultural concerns.
>
> (Waugh 1989: 3)

Waugh's point is certainly an important one. The texts in this study point out repeatedly that *all* subjects are created in ideology, even those who might be considered dominant because male. However, although the literary texts studied here are written by men, there are also marginalized groups within them. Who is to say that Scottish (Alasdair Gray) or Indian (Salman Rushdie) male writers might not also consider themselves as marginal figures?

Both Realism and postmodernism have been examined by critics as period concepts, with specific (though disputed) causes and beginnings. Both have been designated as the products of various stages in the development of capitalism, either caused by its rise, or as evidence of its decline (see, for example: Becker 1980: 8–39; Calinescu 1986: 239–54; Eagleton 1985: 60–73; Jameson 1984: 53–92; Newman 1985). These issues are certainly important ones, but at the risk of a chapter on Realism in Neanderthal man, I have limited my discussion of Realism and postmodernism to *effects* rather than causes.[3]

The "canon" I have chosen is largely British, with the exception of the final chapter which includes a discussion of popular (Canadian and American) culture and Stephen King's novel *Misery*. (There, because I wanted to discuss Realism in popular culture, I had to rely on my (North American) experience of it. Stephen King, though American, was chosen as a typical figure.) Not only has a great deal of work been done on the postmodern American novel, or "Surfiction" to use Federman's term (1975), but recent British postmodern fiction seems to be more closely and more interestingly tied to the Realist tradition. Surfiction such as that of William Gass, Raymond Federman, Ronald Sukenick, or Donald Barthelme plays with the conventions of Realism in a much more overt way. Typographical complexity, as well as obvious and often strident play with the reader, give the Realist conventions much less authority. However, many of the texts in this study firmly install Realist techniques, and in some cases seem at first to *be* Realist texts: Graham Swift's *Waterland* is a good example. It is clear from these texts that postmodernist techniques challenge Realist conventions from within the very conventions they wish to subvert.

Postmodern fiction, then, plays (seriously) with the structures of authority. It exists in the liminal space between power and subversion, which is the space of exploration of this study. The structure of these texts seems to acknowledge that Realism still has control over the way in which literature is read, taught, and evaluated. However, postmodern challenges to Realist conventions suggest that this authority and its relation to experience are at least under interrogation.

Chapter one

Realism and its discontents

Men can do nothing without the make-believe of a beginning. Even Science, the strict measurer, is obliged to start with a make-believe unit, and must fix on a point in the stars' unceasing journey when his sidereal clock shall pretend that time is at Nought. His less accurate grandmother Poetry has always been understood to start in the middle; but on reflection it appears that her proceeding is not very different from his; since Science, too, reckons backwards as well as forwards, divides his unit into billions, and with his clock finger at Nought really sets off *in medias res*. No retrospect will take us to the true beginning; and whether our prologue be in heaven or on earth, it is but a fraction of that all-presupposing fact with which our story sets out.

George Eliot, *Daniel Deronda*, 1967: 35

In Julian Barnes' novel *Flaubert's Parrot*, Geoffrey Braithwaite, a Flaubert enthusiast, tries to identify the "real" stuffed parrot which served as Flaubert's inspiration for Loulou in *Un coeur simple*. Finding the true parrot, he feels, would be tantamount to finding the author's true voice and, as Braithwaite discovers, this is a difficult task. Having found one authentic parrot, he is moved to feel he "had almost known the writer" (Barnes 1984: 16). Having found another, he feels rebuked: "The writer's voice – what makes you think it can be located that easily?" (ibid. 22).

Braithwaite is only intermittently self-conscious about his attempt to find the "true" Flaubert through this and other relics of his life, although he is well aware that Flaubert "forbade posterity to take any personal interest in him" (Barnes 1984: 16). He recognizes that the past is "autobiographical criticism pretending to be parliamentary report" (ibid.: 90), and that the "truth" about Flaubert is as difficult to authenticate as are the various stuffed parrots. Nevertheless, Braithwaite is obsessed by the minutiae of Flaubert's every movement. He tries to reconstruct the past to the extent that he tries to *be* both Flaubert and Louise Colet, Flaubert's mistress. His attempt at scrupulous documentation sometimes extends to the ridiculous. Having read that Flaubert "watched the sun go down over the seas and declared that it resembled a large disc of redcurrant jam" (Barnes 1984: 92), Braithwaite writes to the Grocer's Company to find out if an 1853 pot of Rouennais jam would have been the same color as a modern one. Assured that the color would have been very similar, he writes, if somewhat bashfully, "So at least that's all right: now we can go ahead and confidently imagine the sunset" (Barnes 1984: 93). While his obsession with documentation is almost maniacal where Flaubert's life is concerned, Braithwaite derides with confident irony those critics who try to treat fiction as documentary history:

> I'll remember instead another lecture I once attended, some years ago at the Cheltenham Literary Festival. It was given by a professor from Cambridge, Christopher Ricks, and it was a very shiny performance. His bald head was shiny; his black shoes were shiny; and his lecture was very shiny indeed. Its theme was Mistakes in Literature and Whether They Matter. Yevtushenko, for example, apparently made a howler in one of his poems about the American nightingale. Pushkin was quite wrong about the sort of military dress worn at balls. John Wain was wrong about the Hiroshima pilot. Nabokov was wrong – rather surprising this – about the phonetics of the name Lolita. There were other examples: Coleridge, Yeats and Browning were some of those caught out not knowing a hawk from a handsaw, or not even knowing what a handsaw was in the first place.
>
> (Barnes 1984: 76)

The point of this is that if "the factual side of literature becomes unreliable, then ploys such as irony and fantasy become much harder to use" (ibid.: 77). In other words, the literariness of the text is dependent upon the veracity of the facts.

Interestingly, the novel as a whole plays with precisely this notion. Braithwaite accumulates a vast amount of information about Flaubert, but this knowledge only makes him Flaubert's parrot. For Félicité in *Un coeur simple*, the parrot Loulou has mystical, religious connotations. Finding the "real" parrot, however, will not give Braithwaite any mystical insight into either Flaubert or his fiction. The facts do not lead, as he hopes they will, to truth. *Flaubert's Parrot* uses the Realist convention of historical documentation in order to give the novel an illusion of reality. It does, after all, contain references to real people – Gustave Flaubert, Enid Starkie, Christopher Ricks – and places – Rouen, Trouville, Croisset. That these people exist or existed is verifiable in the "Ricksian" sense. However, they exist in the novel not as objective facts, but as determined by the fictional Braithwaite's perception of them. Indeed, they become fictional constructs, both because of this, and because they are framed within the covers of a novel. Through metafictional techniques the novel creates levels of fiction and "reality" and questions the Realist assumption that truth and reality are absolutes. *Flaubert's Parrot* is typical of contemporary metafictional texts in that, while it challenges Realist conventions, it does so, paradoxically, from within precisely those same conventions. Metafiction often contains its own criticism, and the novels which play with Realist codes criticize, as this one does, their own use of them. More generally, they call into question the basic suppositions made popular by nineteenth-century Realism.

The Realist movement endorsed a particular way of looking at art and life as though there was a direct correspondence between the two. The critical method, then, involved charting the similarities and differences between experiential reality and the artist's transcription of it, assuming, of course, that experiential reality was common to all. Geoffrey Braithwaite and "Christopher Ricks" in *Flaubert's Parrot* are in this sense Realists. In fact, however, Realism has little to do with reality. It is, rather, a critical construct which developed in a particular social and ideological context. Nevertheless, some manifestations of the Realist movement still have currency, particularly, as *Flaubert's Parrot* suggests, the notion that art is a means to truth because the artist has a privileged insight into a common sense of what constitutes "reality." In a sense, even Geoffrey Braithwaite's touristy enthusiasm is the result of this suspect belief. His example, however, is followed by all those similar enthusiasts who look for Michael Henchard's house in Dorchester or Romeo and Juliet paraphernalia in Verona. Recently, the English National Trust decided to refashion the Suffolk landscape to make it resemble Constable's painting *The Haywain*, and a series of huge timbers found in the River Stour have become news items because they may be from the boat that inspired Constable's *Boat Building Near Flatford Mill*. All of these are examples of a fascination with Realism.

As a literary movement,[1] Realism was first formulated in mid-nineteenth-century France, although it soon gained currency in England and the rest of Europe. The term first appears in France in 1826 when a writer in *Mercure Français* comments that "this literary doctrine, which gains ground every day and will lead to faithful imitation not of the masterworks of art but of the originals offered by nature, could very well be called realism. According to some indications it will be the literature of the 19th century, the literature of the true" (Wellek 1966: vol. 4:1).

There is no formal manifesto of Realism in the way that the prefaces to the 1802 and 1805 editions of the *Lyrical Ballads* set the scope and limits of English Romanticism. However, a conjunction of publications and events in France in the mid-1850s made Realism a topic for often heated debate:

> It was in 1855 that the painter Courbet placed the sign "Du Réalisme" over the door of his one man show. In 1856 Edmond Duranty began a short-lived review called *Réalisme*, and in the following year Champfleury, an enthusiastic supporter of Courbet and the new literature, brought out a volume of critical discussions entitled *Le Réalisme*. The term was launched though its meaning was still to be defined.
>
> (Becker 1963: 7)

In England, Thackeray was called "chief of the Realist school" in *Fraser's* in 1851 (Stang 1961: 148), and an 1853 article in *Westminster Review* discussed Balzac in association with Realism

(Becker 1963: 7). The *Oxford English Dictionary* cites volume four of Ruskin's *Modern Painters* as first using the term "realism" in 1856. It is clear, then, that by the mid-1850s Realism had become topical either as a "rallying cry or a term of disparagement" (Hemmings 1974: 162).

The theoretical premise of Realism is that art should eschew the "idealist metaphysics" (Becker 1963: 6) of Romanticism, and portray instead "things as they really are, in the sense of portraying objectively and concretely the observable details of actual life" (Kaminsky 1974: 217). This apparently simple dictate creates such innumerable difficulties that it has become a commonplace that Realism is one of the most problematic of terms. One of the major problems is that the Realists appear to have wanted to create a formula for the literal transcription of reality into art. This very premise is contradictory since, as soon as there exists a frame for reality, anything that is within that frame ceases to be "reality" and becomes artifact. A good example of this problem is illustrated by Magritte's painting *The Human Condition I* (1934). Within the painting is a painting on an easel which overlaps a landscape seen through a window. The painting-within-the-painting is an exact continuation of the view, and so it appears that there are two levels: the "real" view and the painted copy. As Robert Hughes points out in *The Shock of the New*:

> the play between image and reality suggests that the real world is only a construction of mind. We know that if we moved the easel, the view through the window would be the same as the one shown on the painting within the painting; but because the whole scene is locked in the immobility and permanence of a larger painting, we cannot know it.
>
> (Hughes 1980: 247)

Because the "real" view is framed within a painting, it ceases to be real and becomes instead an imaginative construct. Even the very medium itself is not transparent, and therefore prevents any possibility of art mirroring reality. Indeed, Linda Nochlin comments that no matter how objective the artist's vision is, the visible world must be changed in order to translate it on to the flat surface of the canvas: "The artist's perception is therefore inevitably conditioned by the physical properties of paint and linseed no less than by his knowledge and technique – even by his choice of brush-strokes – in conveying three-dimensional space and form on to a two-dimensional picture plane" (Nochlin 1976: 15).

The nineteenth century, of course, was not the first to concern itself with the relationship of life and art. M. H. Abrams, in *The Mirror and the Lamp*, points out that the "mimetic orientation – the explanation of art as essentially an imitation of aspects in the universe – was probably the most primitive aesthetic theory" (1953: 8). Plato banishes the poet from the Republic (10: 606E), because his art is thrice removed from the truth (10: 595C): "painting and imitation generally carry out their work far from the truth and have to do with that part within us that is remote from the truth, and that the two arts are companions and friends of nothing wholesome or true" (10: 602C). That the poet deals in untruths is further compounded because he imitates things whose essence he knows nothing about, and does so in such a way as to delude (10: 602C) and corrupt good citizens (10: 605A). Plato's reasons for his mistrust of the poet are social rather than aesthetic, and nineteenth-century Realism tends to be closer to Aristotelian mimesis than Platonic imitation. However, Plato's mistrust of literature as a form of lying is echoed in the nineteenth century, and is related to the Realist and Naturalist desire to make literature conform to so-called "neutral" scientific laws and "objective" historical documentation.

In *The Function of Mimesis and its Decline*, John D. Boyd, S.J. writes: "What organic union there is in the Western critical tradition of poetry's needed realism and autonomy is largely derived from Aristotle" (1968: 18). However, Boyd distinguishes between Aristotelian "realism" as a search into human action, and the "vogue since the nineteenth century of applying the word to literature that deals largely with techniques akin to the photographic" (ibid.: 24). As this suggests, for Aristotle, as for Plato, the poet is an imitator. The imitation, however, is, as Aristotle suggests in *Poetics*, of "men who are doing something" (2: 48a1) rather than of shadows of truth. Primarily, for Aristotle, the poet is a creator. He does not merely mirror reality, but instead creates highly structured plots (7: 51a16; 50b21) not about what *has* happened but about "what might happen and what is possible according to probability or necessity" (9: 51a36). Within the conditions of the probable and the necessary, the poet has some creative choices about the subject of his imitation. He or she must always imitate "one of the three aspects of things: either as they were or are, or as men say they are and they seem to be, or as they ought to be" (25: 60b6). According to Aristotle, then, the poet is a fiction maker, not an historian. Poetry is, in fact, more serious than history, since while poetry deals with universals, history deals with each thing for itself (9: 51a36). Thus Aristotle is less concerned with documentation than with artistry: "it is less serious for a painter not to know that a female deer has no horns than to represent one inartistically" (25: 60b23). For painters as for writers, the mimetic issue has never really disappeared.[2]

In Stendhal's *Scarlet and Black*, the novel is described as a genre which should be democratic in subject-matter and objective in style:

> a novel is a mirror journeying down the high road. Sometimes it reflects to your view the azure blue of heaven, sometimes the mire in the puddles on the road below. And the man who carries the mirror in his sack will be accused by you of being immoral! His mirror reflects the mire, and you blame the mirror! Blame rather the high road in which the puddle lies, and still more the inspector of roads and highways who lets the water stand there and the puddle form.
>
> (Stendhal 1830: 365–6)

The Goncourt brothers, in the preface to *Germinie Lacerteux*, were equally insistent about the all-inclusiveness of the novel: "Living in the nineteenth century, in a time of universal suffrage, democracy, and liberalism, we asked ourselves whether what we called 'the lower classes' did not have a right to the Novel" (1963: 118). Their "democracy," like that of the other exponents of Realism, purported to embrace not only the lower classes, but also those "to which the past century gave that broad and encompassing name, *Humanity*" (Goncourt 1963: 119). Thus, the province of the novel expands to include not only the drawing room, but also the ordinary, the ugly, and the low. Whatever, in fact, can be observed is a fit subject for the novel. In this particular aspect of Realism, there is some correspondence between theory and fiction. This is often, particularly in English novels of the period, not the case. Many of the novels, however, make explicit comments, either in prefaces or within the text, about the use of characters and situations drawn from everyday life. George Eliot in *Adam Bede*, for example, begins her chapter "In Which the Story Pauses a Little," with a narrative address to the reader: "'This Rector of Broxton is little better than a pagan' I hear one of my readers exclaim. 'How much more edifying it would have been if you had made him give Arthur some truly spiritual advice. You might have put into his mouth the most beautiful things – quite as good as reading a sermon'" (Eliot 1980: 221). In answer to this implied reader, Eliot defends a faithful reflection of ordinary life:

> Certainly I could if I held it in the highest vocation of the novelist to represent things as they never have been and never will be. Then, of course, I might refashion life and character entirely after my own liking; I might select the most unexceptional type of clergyman, and put my own admirable opinions into his mouth on all occasions. But it happens, on the contrary, that my strongest effort is to avoid any such arbitrary picture, and to give a faithful account of men and things as they have mirrored themselves in my mind. The mirror is doubtless defective; the outline will sometimes be disturbed, the reflection faint or confused; but I feel as much bound to tell you as precisely as I can what that reflection is, as if I were in the witness box narrating my experience on oath.
>
> (Eliot 1980: 221)

Ironically, while she defends this one aspect of Realism in her content, Eliot contravenes others in her form. One of these is the doctrine of impersonality which developed as part of a larger concern for objectivity. As we will see, a Realist text in the sense that it was, and is, defined by Realist critics, does not exist. Novelists such as Walter Scott, Thackeray, Trollope, Charlotte Brontë, to name but a few, have all been hailed as writers of Realist texts. Each of their texts, however, like *Adam Bede*, contains self-conscious moments which in themselves undermine Realist dictates. It is interesting that even the passage from *Scarlet and Black* quoted (pp. 365–6), often considered an exemplum of Realist thought, occurs in a chapter which not only discusses Mathilde as an imaginative construct, but in which the narrator laments that he might well be accused of impropriety in the creation of her passions.

The Realists believed that perception could be pure, and that the facts in a novel should speak for themselves without authorial commentary and its attendant reader manipulation (see Becker 1963: 28). In a chapter on "Realist Drama" in *Old Saws and Modern Instances*, W. L. Courtney is even insistent on removing artistic language from a purportedly Realist work: "Realism means above all else a devotion to the bare and explicit truth of human life and human character, and the avoidance of all romantic or poetic devices for obscuring the main issues" (1918: 189). Clearly the self-consciousness of authorial intervention like George Eliot's subverts this assumption, particularly because Eliot fictionalizes her own identity by appearing in the novel at all. A more serious crime against Realism by supposedly Realist writers is that, by commenting on the process of the novel, as well as in drawing attention to its existence as an artifact, they are emphatically in the realm of art, not of "life." Thackeray ends *Vanity Fair*, for example, by doing precisely this: "Come, children, let us shut up the box and the puppets, for our play is played out" (1968: 797).

The doctrine of impersonality, as well as other Realist theories, is often espoused by authors in their critical writings while their novels attest to an opposing practice. It would seem that many modern literary critics ignore this point. Robert Alter, among others, sees the tradition of the self-conscious novel as one which is in eclipse in the nineteenth century:

> The realist desire to register the minute oscillations and effects of historical change leads novelists away from the exploration of fiction as artifice for a variety of reasons. . . . The imaginative involvement with history, in any case, is the main cause of an almost complete eclipse of the self-conscious novel during the nineteenth century.
>
> (Alter 1975: 88–9)

It is easy to sympathize with Chris Baldick who, in a review article in the *Times Literary Supplement*, writes:

> Among today's theoreticians of post-modern writing, some remarkable legends about the Dark Ages of nineteenth-century

realist fiction have been allowed to gain currency. It can now almost go without saying that the objective of realist fiction was to inhibit any questioning of the world, to induce complacency and stupefying ideological amnesia.

(Baldick 1985: 295)

It could certainly be argued that this is the case with nineteenth- (and twentieth-) century Realist theories, but even the most cursory glance at a nineteenth-century novel will reveal that, for fiction, this is not the case. Novels of the period which are even now reputed to be examples of high Realism – particularly those by George Eliot, Gustave Flaubert, and Henry James – are certainly aware of their own artifice and their own processes, even if their authors, in their non-fiction texts, take a different view.

Gustave Flaubert wrote repeatedly in letters and articles about the need for novelistic impersonality and impartiality:

The illusion (if there is one) comes . . . from the impersonality of the work. It is one of my principles that you must not *write yourself*. The artist ought to be in his work like God in creation, invisible and omnipotent. He should be felt every where [*sic*] but not seen. Art ought, moreover, to rise above personal feelings and nervous susceptibilities! It is time to give it the precision of the physical sciences, by means of a pitiless method!

(Flaubert 1963: 94–5)

Although Flaubert's texts are not interrupted by intrusions of the type that Eliot uses, Flaubert is clearly *not* an impersonal author. Narrative comments in *Madame Bovary* such as "Emma *soiled* her hands with the *refuse* of old lending libraries" (1975: 50, my emphasis), make it apparent that neither impersonality nor scientific objectivity is applied to Emma Bovary's reading.

Henry James also wrote about the necessity of impersonality in "The Art of Fiction," and he was vitriolic about authorial intrusion such as that practised by Trollope:

Certain accomplished novelists have a habit of giving them- selves away which must often bring tears to the eyes of people who take their fiction seriously . . . Trollope . . . in a di- gression concedes to the reader that he and this trusting friend are only "making believe". He admits that the events he narrates have not really happened and that he can give his narrative any turn the reader may like best. Such a betrayal of a sacred office seems to me, I confess, a terrible crime. . . . It implies that the novelist is less occupied in looking for the truth . . . than the historian. . . .

(James 1957: 46–7)

There is an assumption here which is common to Realist thought: that the novel is, or should be, an unmanipulated, natural chain of events. Yet, even in James' novels, there is a central intelligence or narrative voice which clearly directs and manipulates the reader rather than letting events "happen naturally." In Chapter forty-two of *The Portrait of a Lady*, for example, the omniscient narrator sees into Isabel Archer's thoughts. This implies an authorial presence as much as do authoritative first-person directives and comments to the reader:

> Very often, however, she felt afraid, and it would come over her, as I have intimated, that she had deceived him at the very first. . . . As I have said, she believed she was not defiant, and what could be better proof of it than that she should linger half the night, trying to persuade herself that there was no reason why Pansy shouldn't be married as you would put a letter in the post office?

(James 1977: 433, 435)

A correlative of objectivity and impersonality is the Realist concern with documentation and fact. This is certainly part of the belief that the novel should mirror the world, and through this impersonal mirroring show "truth." It is a common Realist sentiment that fiction is to be mistrusted unless it pretends to be something else. As Leslie Stephen argued: "there is certainly a good deal to be said for the thesis that all fiction is really a kind of lying and that art in general is a luxurious indulgence, to which we have no right while crime and disease are rampant in the outer world" (1874–9: vol. 4: 73). Henry James felt that the novel should be akin to an historical document. In "The Art of Fiction" he wrote that: "the subject matter of fiction is stored up . . . in documents and records and if it will not give itself away, as they say in California, it must speak with assurance, with the tone of the historian" (1957: 35). Other writers were influenced by the scientific method, and sought to make the novel as objective as they perceived science to be. Thus Zola argues in "The Experimental Novel" for a type of fiction which would be akin to a scientific experiment (1963: 162–96). In the preface to the second edition of *Thérèse Raquin* he describes his scientific purpose: "I hope that by now it is becoming clear that my object has been first and foremost a scientific one. . . . It simply applies to two living bodies the analytical method that surgeons apply to corpses" (1867: 22, 23).

This particular obsession, that fiction should pretend to be or aspire to be fact was not, of course, new, nor was it unique to the Realists. J. Hillis Miller points out that although the novel most often masks itself as a form of history, it has also "displaced" itself in various other ways as, for example, a collection of letters, memoirs or edited documents, an old manuscript found in a trunk or bottle, journalism or travel notes (Miller 1974: 456). These devices validate "lying" literature because they create the illusion that there is a one-to-one correspondence between the novel and history (ibid.: 456). Several now untenable assumptions are clear, here. The first of these is that "empirical reality" is objectively observable through pure perception. The second is that there can exist a direct transcription from "reality" to novel. Implicit in this is the idea that language is transparent, that "reality" creates language and not the reverse. Zola voiced a common hypothesis in "The Experimental Novel," that language is "nothing but logic, a natural and scientific construction" (1963: 192). Finally, there is the notion that there is a common, shared sense of both "reality" and "truth." Fernand Desnoyers has a doctrinaire tone when he writes: "Since the word truth puts everybody in agreement and since everybody approves of the word, even liars, one must admit that, without being an apologist for ugliness and evil, realism has the right to represent whatever exists and whatever we see" (1963: 81). Similarly, Henry James, in *The Art of the Novel*, explicitly describes reality as "the things we cannot *not* know sooner or later, in one way or another; it being but one of the accidents of our hampered state, and one of the instances of their quantity and number that particular instances have not yet come our way" (1962: 31). This, of course, assumes an objective, external essence which, in time, will become readily apparent to all. It becomes impossible, then, to criticize James, for his own subversion of Realism, his criticism, or anything else, since such a criticism will only reflect the extent to which the critic's state is "hampered."

The dictates of objectivity, impersonality, and documentation would seem to make of the novelist a kind of Thomas Gradgrind constantly in search of fact. Indeed, it was the author in whom Realist criticism had its greatest interest. The pervasive moral element of Realism, particularly in England (see, for example, Williams 1975: xiii), explains this. If there is a common understanding of "reality" and the author tries to reflect this in his or her novel, then it follows that the criticism of the novel must concentrate on the accuracy of the reflection. Since for the Realists, language is "natural," the artistic *process* of the novel does not play a significant role for the critic. If, therefore, the critic sees a discrepancy between the author's "objective" view and his or her own (and the chances of this not happening are remote), then the fault must be in the author. As Aristotle does in the *Poetics* (4: 48b4), Realist theorists insist that the aim of art is to instruct. The morality of the author is, therefore, highly important, and it is for this reason that the Realists often wrote, and still write, biographical criticism as well as rules for, and criticism of, authors' moral virtues. The essential equation is that "good" men will produce "good" art. Thomas Carlyle, for example, was interested in morality and fact to the extent that his literary criticism takes on the tone of the pulpit. Eventually, his belief that "the smallest historical fact" is more impressive than the "grandest *fictitious* event" (Carlyle 1899: vol. 3: 54), led him away from the study of "lying" literature to the study of "reality" through history. For Carlyle, good art depends on the poet's ability to see the real, and to transcribe it in a "memorable" almost magical way. However, in "Biography" he writes:

> one grand, invaluable secret there is . . . which includes all the rest, and what is comfortable, lies clearly in every man's power: *To have an open loving heart, and what follows from the possession of such.* Truly, it has been said, emphatically in these days ought it to be repeated: A loving Heart is the beginning of all Knowledge, this it is that opens the whole mind, quickens every faculty of the intellect to do its fit work,

that of *knowing*; and therefrom, by sure consequence, of *vividly uttering forth*.

(Carlyle 1899: vol. 3: 57)

Like Carlyle, John Ruskin believes in the necessary moral quality of the artist. Although he is primarily an art critic, his *Modern Painters* developed an influential aesthetic theory. For Ruskin, the ideal painter is a man who sees only loveliness: "there is no Evil in his eyes; – only Good and that which displays Good" (1903–12a vol. 4: 386). In "The Queen of the Air," he is insistent that "Great art is the expression of the mind of a great man, and mean art, that of the want of mind of a weak man" (1903–12b: 19: 389).

It is easy to see how this kind of criticism loses sight of the processes and structures of art except in so far as the art is the reflection of a good man whose example will offer appropriate moral instruction to the reader. Art develops, then, the status of religion, and the artist becomes a moral guide. This is certainly one of the several aspects of Realism which has intruded into the twentieth century.[3] In *Literary Theory*, Terry Eagleton discusses the rise of English studies as a correlative of the decline of religion, which scientific discovery and social change were causing to be questioned as an authority (1983: 22-3). Literature appeared to be an apt replacement as Eagleton points out:

Like religion, literature works primarily by emotion and experience, and so was admirably well-fitted to carry through the ideological task which religion left off. Indeed by our own time literature has become effectively identical with the opposite of analytical thought and conceptual inquiry; whereas scientists, philosophers and political theorists are saddled with these drably discursive pursuits, students of literature occupy the more prized territory of feeling and experience. Whose experience and what kinds of feeling, is a different question. Literature from Arnold onwards is the enemy of "ideological dogma", an attitude which might have come as a surprise to Dante, Milton and Pope.

(Eagleton 1983: 26)

It seems here that religion is merely a sham copy of poetry, and Arnold certainly gave "the greatest poetry" an enormous responsibility in his search for what Douglas Bush calls "a faith of enduring validity" (Bush 1971: 85). It is possible that this replacement of religion by poetry could have evolved in part from, or is at least similar to, the Realist view that art corresponds directly to life, and that its moral and eternal verities are apprehended by common sense.

In *The Social Mission of English Criticism*, Chris Baldick points out that the responsibility given to poetry by Arnold is equalled by his insistence on the "social and cultural duties" (1985: 19) of criticism. Baldick argues that, for Arnold, the critic has "the task of seeking out the best materials in all branches of intellectual activity" (ibid.: 20). Yet paradoxically, "practical criticism" is to be viewed with suspicion. The critic must remain outside ideology so as eventually to make the world a better place. In "The Function of Criticism at the Present Time" Arnold writes:

> A polemical practical criticism makes men blind even to the ideal imperfection of their practice, makes them willingly assert its ideal perfection, in order the better to secure it against attack; and clearly this is narrowing and baneful for them. If they were reassured on the practical side, speculative consider-ations of ideal perfection they might be brought to entertain, and their spiritual horizon would thus gradually widen.
>
> (Arnold 1970: 144)

He wonders then: "Where shall we find language innocent enough, how shall we make the spotless purity of our intentions evident enough . . .?" (Ibid.: 147). Baldick points out that, in Arnold's search for an innocent, transparent language, he elevates critical discourse to a position of privilege outside "partial or partisan considerations" (1985: 25). Indeed criticism here could well be described as following the Realist dictates for fiction, particularly those of objectivity, transparent language, pure perceptions, and, of course, moral instruction.

These ideas are of particular importance for literary studies since F.R. Leavis, arguably Arnold's critical heir, universalized Arnold's notions of critical and literary value through his promotion of English studies at Cambridge. Terry Eagleton rightly comments in *Literary Theory* that the fact remains that English students in England today are "Leavisites" whether they know it or not, irremediably altered by that historic intervention. There is no more need to be a card-carrying Leavisite today than there is to be a card-carrying Copernican: that current has entered the bloodstream of English studies in England as Copernicus reshaped our astronomical beliefs, has become a form of spontaneous critical wisdom as deep-seated as our conviction that the earth moves round the sun.

(Eagleton 1983: 31)

Like Arnold, Leavis sees criticism as an act of defending Culture against a decline in traditional values. As he argues in *Culture and Environment*, the effects of the machine and mechanization have destroyed the "old ways of life" (Leavis and Thompson 1933: 3), and the advent of influences such as film, newspapers, and advertizing is a danger to the "possibilities of training taste and sensibility" (ibid.: 1) in the classroom. Thus, in *For Continuity*, he pleads for a critical minority who will guard and propagate what he calls the "consciousness of the race":

Upon this minority depends our power of profiting by the finest human experience of the past; they keep alive the subtlest and most perishable parts of tradition. Upon them depend the implicit standards that order the finer living of an age, the sense that this is worth more than that, this rather than that is the direction in which to go, that the centre is here rather than there. In their keeping . . . is the language . . . upon which fine living depends. . . . By "culture" I mean the use of such a language. I do not suppose myself to have produced a tight definition, but the account, I think, will be recognized as adequate by anyone who is likely to read this pamphlet.

(Leavis 1933: 14–15)

Leavis echoes Arnold's and Ruskin's view that good men produce good art. Therefore, the novelists in *The Great Tradition* are distinguished by a "vital capacity for experience, a kind of reverent openness before life, and a marked moral intensity" (Leavis 1972: 18). Through their novels, these men and women of "genius" "change the possibilities of art for practitioners and readers," and are "significant in terms of the human awareness they promote; awareness of the possibilities of life" (ibid.: 10). Just what Leavis means by this is notoriously unclear (but the admission of the extent to which it is unclear merely reflects the reader's lack of a moral intensity which would allow him or her to understand it). His system, then, like Henry James' definition of the real, is closed and circular. The author's "genius" as well as the reader's response are questions of how deeply they both Feel Life. Literature can make the reader a "better" person, but only if he or she shares the capacity for moral seriousness with both the author and Dr Leavis. Eagleton responds to this in *Literary Theory* with the following:

> When the Allied troops moved into the concentration camps some years after the founding of *Scrutiny*, to arrest commandants who had whiled away their leisure hours with a volume of Goethe, it appeared that someone had some explaining to do. If reading literature made you a better person, then it was hardly in the direct ways that this case at its most euphoric had imagined.
>
> (Eagleton 1983: 35)

Obviously this is a quip, but it addresses one of the fundamental problems with Leavisian criticism. Leavis believes in the transcendental value of literature as a moral teacher and therefore, in a common sense of what life, value, and morality mean – at least among the cultural elite referred to above. This is reflected as much in his content as in his method of criticism. While some of his critical comments rely on close readings, much of his criticism consists of quoting large passages from the "great" authors, with the assumption that his response and the reader's will be the same. Leavis was vehemently opposed to any theorizing which might have clarified his terms. In "Literary Criticism and Philosophy," in fact, he responded to René Wellek's complaint about precisely this issue:

> The business of the literary critic is to attain a peculiar completeness of response and to observe a peculiarly strict relevance in developing his response into commentary; he must be on his guard against abstracting improperly from what is in front of him and against any premature or irrelevant generalizing – of it or from it. His first concern is to enter into

17

possession of the given poem (let us say) in its concrete fullness, and his constant concern is never to lose his completeness of possession with that fullness of response.

(Leavis 1937: 61)

It is clear that Leavis shares many of the Realist assumptions such as the value of biographical criticism, the direct correspondence between art and life, and the transparency of language which is merely a medium to reflect the author's "genius" and "vitality." We see this in *The Great Tradition* in which he praises Dickens for his ability to capture the "real":

To the question how the reconciling is done – there is much more diversity in *Hard Times* than these references to dialogue suggest – the answer can be given by pointing to the astonishing and irresistible richness of life that characterizes the book everywhere. It meets us everywhere, unstrained and natural, in the prose. Out of such prose a great variety of presentations can arise congenially with equal vividness. There they are, unquestionably "real." It goes back to an extraordinary energy of perception and registration in Dickens. . . . His flexibility is that of a richly poetic art of the word. He doesn't write "poetic prose"; he writes with a poetic force of evocation, registering with the responsiveness of a genius of verbal expression what he so sharply sees and feels. In fact, by texture, imaginative mode, symbolic method, and the resulting concentration, *Hard Times* affects us as belonging with formally poetic works.

(Leavis 1972: 267).

Through Leavis many of the tenets of literary Realism immigrated to the twentieth century and are still in vogue. Although some of the modern critics do see Realism as a critical construct, influenced by social and economic forces, others still see it as a means to truth.[4] The 1961 debate between René Wellek and E. B. Greenwood in *Neophilologus* is a good example of the continuing interest in, and confusion about, Realism. These two critics represent diametrically opposed views about both Realism and art. Wellek, in "The Concept of Realism in Literary Scholarship," surveys various conflicting theories of Realism, and notes the rise of "socialist realism" as a contributing factor to the continuation of the modern debate. He sees Realism as a "period concept" (Wellek 1961: 10), whose dictates will "not be completely fulfilled by any single work" (ibid.: 16). Above all, Realism is a set of conventions and, as Wellek points out, this subverts its claim that it can "penetrate directly into life and reality" (1961: 17). Indeed, one of the problems is that it might, and sometimes does, "lose all distinction between art and the conveyance of information" (ibid.: 17–18). In conclusion, Wellek makes the important point that the theory of Realism is "bad aesthetics" (1961: 18) because it denies that all art is "'making' and is a world in itself of illusion and symbolic forms" (ibid. 18).

E. B. Greenwood attempts to take Wellek to task for his concept of Realism, arguing from a point of view which echoes those of Arnold and Leavis. In particular, Greenwood denies that the isolation of Realism as a period concept is appropriate since this suggests that Realism is merely a tool, rather than a perennial epistemological concern. Instead, he argues, Realism lies in the "artistic rendering of a universal truth about human nature" (Greenwood 1962: 90). While he agrees with Wellek that literature is artifact, not documentation of reality, this artifact is "felt to be truer and more 'real'" (ibid.: 90) than reality. The major point of contention arises from Wellek's belief that the conventions of Realism *prevent* it from penetrating into life. In contrast, Greenwood argues that Realism implies a necessary connection between art and life, and it is this connection which gives art its value (1962: 94). Greenwood's own concept of Realism is that it is the "truth about the real world" (ibid.: 94), a truth which is "personal, yet universal" (ibid.: 95). Indeed, a "piece of art is good *because* it is true" (ibid.: 96), and criticism involves a judgement about just how true it is. Finally, Realism is the "assertion of art's normality, rationality and morality, in brief of art's humanity," and its forms and devices are designed "to mediate a qualitative and synthetic (as opposed to quantitative and analytic) apprehension of life" (Greenwood 1962: 96). For Greenwood, as for Leavis, art is a product whose language and conventions are merely a means to communicate value. More than 100 years, then, after the inception of Realism as a school of thought, some of what we might now call its most untenable assumptions are still widely held.

Thomas Carlyle writes in "The Death of Goethe" that "the

Word of man (the uttered Thought of man) is still a magic formula whereby he rules the world" (1899: vol. 2: 377). This notion, that words have a "magic" relationship to the objects they represent, is one which twentieth-century structural–linguistic theories have called into question. Particularly important here are the theories of Ferdinand de Saussure, delivered as a series of lectures at the University of Geneva from 1906–1911. The *Course in General Linguistics* was collected from his students' notes and published posthumously in 1915. Saussure's most influential premise is that the relationship between the word in its graphic or spoken form (signifier), and the thing it represents (signified), is a purely arbitrary one. In the English language, for example, the four black marks T-R-E-E, or their sound equivalent, signify "tree," but there is no eternal, magical correspondence between the two. Historically and culturally English speakers agree that these marks indicate some sort of vegetation with a trunk and leaves. However, to assume that the correspondence between word and thing is natural is to forget that in other languages the same concept is signified by an entirely different signifier. Compare, for example, *arbre* in French or *arbor* in Latin (Saussure 1915: 65). There is no reason why this type of vegetation should not be called "blip," except that cultural agreement has decreed otherwise. Saussure's own analogy for this comes from chess:

> Take a knight for instance. By itself is it an element in the game? Certainly not, for by its material make-up – outside its square and the other conditions of the game – it means nothing to the player; it becomes a real, concrete element only when endowed with value and wedded to it. Suppose that the piece happens to be destroyed or lost during a game. Can it be replaced by an equivalent piece? Certainly. Not only another knight but even a figure shorn of any resemblance to a knight can be declared identical provided the same value is attributed to it. We see then that in semiological systems like language, where elements hold each other in equilibrium in accordance with fixed rules, the notion of identity blends with that of value and *vice versa*.

(Saussure 1915: 110)

Words themselves are distinguished from other words not by

their descriptive prowess, but by their difference from other words:

> a difference generally implies positive terms between which the difference is set up; but in language there are only differences *without positive terms*. Whether we take the signified or the signifier, language has neither ideas nor sounds that existed before the linguistic system, but only conceptual and phonic differences that have issued from the system. The idea of phonic substance that a sign contains is of less importance than the other signs that surround it. Proof of this is that the value of a term may be modified without either its meaning or its sound being affected, solely because a neighboring term has been modified.
>
> (Saussure 1915: 120)

Saussure's emphasis, then, is on the *constructedness* of meaning. Linguistic structures determine our perception of reality so that meaning cannot exist independently of language (Norris 1982: 4; Saussure 1915: 65). Stendhal's description of the novel as a mirror walking down the road is, in light of this, inadequate because it assumes that "ready-made ideas exist before words" (Saussure 1915: 65). Instead, structuralists argue, "our knowledge of things is insensibly structured by the systems of code and convention which alone enable us to classify and organize the chaotic flow of experience" (Norris 1982: 4). Literature in structuralist terms can no longer be seen as a natural emanation from a mysteriously inspired, moral mind. Indeed, the gain of structuralist theory is the demystification of literature as an especially privileged discourse since structures, codes, and conventions are found just as much in literature as in Literature (see Eagleton 1983: 106–7). Structuralism challenges the common-sense view that "what is most 'real' is what is experienced, and that the home of this rich, subtle, complex experience is literature itself. Like Freud, it exposes the shocking truth that our most intimate experience is the effect of a structure" (Eagleton 1983: 109).

If meaning is socially constructed and plural rather than naturally existing and single, then the author is as much at the mercy of linguistic structures as the reader or critic. While Realists saw the author as the producer of meaning and morality, post-Saussurian critics look for meaning in a cocreative relationship between the text and the reader. The first important attack on the Realist reliance on biographical criticism, however, is not influenced by structural linguists, although the later direction of reader-response and post-structural criticisms owes something to the vehemence of the New Critical position on authorial influence. W. K. Wimsatt and Monroe C. Beardsley proclaimed in "The Intentional Fallacy" the New Critical point of view that "the design or intention of the author is neither available nor desirable as a standard for judging the success of a work of literary art" (1954b: 3). Even when an author's position is known, through biography or direct statement, it has nothing to do with critical inquiry (ibid.: 18). According to Wimsatt and Beardsley, the "intention school" is misguided in searching for a poetic correlative of terms such as sincerity, genuineness, spontaneity, or fidelity (ibid.: 9). These terms have to do with the poet, not the poem. Instead, they suggest a more specifically critical vocabulary – unity, subtlety, function, integrity – for dealing with the poem as a discrete entity. Because language is public, they argue, the poem is also public, and therefore has little to do with the private or idiosyncratic (Wimsatt and Beardsley 1954b: 10) details of the poet's life: "the poem is not the critic's own and not the author's (it is detached from the author at birth and goes about the world beyond his power to intend about it or control it)" (ibid.: 5). It is the poem as it appears on the page, then, which is of primary importance to the New Critics. Meaning (and even morality) is determined by the poem alone, and no external factors brought to bear on it by author or critic are of value:

> We inquire now not about origins, nor about effects, but about the work so far as it can be considered by itself as a body of meaning. Neither the qualities of the author's mind nor the effects of a poem upon a reader's mind should be confused with the moral quality of the meaning expressed by the poem itself.
>
> (Wimsatt and Beardsley 1954b: 87)

The other side of the New Critical coin is "The Affective Fallacy." As Wimsatt and Beardsley describe it, it is a "confusion between the poem and its *results* (what it *is* and what it *does*). . . . It begins by trying to derive the standard of criticism from the psychological effects of the poem and ends in impressionism and relativism" (1954a: 21). In the case of both the affective and the intentional fallacies, they argue, the poem itself tends to disappear as an object of critical judgement. One of the reasons for the affective fallacy is that emotion is indeterminate: "The report of some readers . . . that a poem or story induces in them vivid images, intense feelings, or heightened consciousness, is neither anything which can be refuted nor anything which it is possible for the objective critic to take into account" (Wimsatt and Beardsley 1954a: 32). What the objective critic can take into account, however, is that the poem represents emotion as an object whose patterns are available for study. Indeed, poems are in themselves representations and communications of information about attitudes and patterns of emotion: "in the poet's finely contrived objects of emotion and in other works of art the historian finds his most reliable evidence about the emotions of antiquity. . . . In short, though cultures have changed and will change, poems remain and explain" (Wimsatt and Beardsley 1954a: 39).

In the context of my argument here, the problem with New Criticism is that while it attacks the Realist reliance on biography as a critical tool, it none the less echoes the Realist position that the text is a univocal "icon" or "oracle." It is a static product, and no anterior affect or knowledge, with the exception of that provided by a dictionary, can be considered in a New Critical analysis. The text for the New Critics, then, would seem to exist only as a spatial figure, disconnected in its wanderings from any social or historical context (Eagleton 1983: 48).

The possibility of the sort of objective, pure perception sought after by the New Critics was called into question by the rise of reader-response criticism in the 1960s. Reception theorists and structuralists, particularly Roland Barthes, turned their attention from the author as moral teacher, and the literary work as icon, to the interaction *between* text and reader. Reader-response criticism seeks to take issue with the authority of a univocal textual meaning. Since texts do not "mean" by themselves, "meaning" has to be brought to them by a shared creative process between text and reader. Each reader will bring to a text different, culturally and pedagogically determined, knowledges, and thus interpret a text in a variety of ways. Thus, as Susan Suleiman argues in her introduction to *The Reader in the Text*, the move away from the New Critical emphasis on textual autonomy has been brought about by a recognition of the "relevance of context" (Suleiman and Crosman 1980: 5). It is, equally, a challenge to purely objective criticism. Indeed, as Jane Tompkins points out in *Reader-Response Criticism*, "Reader-response critics would argue that a poem cannot be understood apart from its results. Its 'effects', psychological and otherwise, are essential to any accurate description of its meaning, since that meaning has no effective existence outside of its realization in the mind of the reader" (1981: ix). At its best, reader-response examines not only the responses of the reader, but, more importantly, the status of the literary text itself as self-conscious and multivocal. It reminds us that language itself is plural. Gerald Prince, for example, in "Notes on the Text as Reader" looks at the variety of cultural and textual codes which can influence interpretation:

> reading a narrative implies organizing it and interpreting it in terms of several more or less complex (sub-) codes. The reader frequently has to determine the connotations of a given passage, the symbolic dimensions of a given event, the hermeneutic function of a given situation, and so on. Reading interludes provide him with certain specific sets of connotations; they make *some* symbolic dimensions explicit; they define the hermeneutic status of *some* situations. In short, they may allow for rest periods, as it were, and may facilitate understanding.
>
> (Prince 1980: 239)

Reader-response criticism at its worst, however, partakes of the same authoritative stance as do the New Critics in insisting on an ideal reader (usually the critic) who will determine a single meaning. In "Literary Competence," for example, Jonathan Culler is much less tentative than Prince:

> the analyst "must convince the reader that he knows what he is talking about" – must make him see the appropriateness of the effects in question – and "must coax the reader into seeing that the cause he names does, in fact, produce the effect which is

experienced; otherwise they will not seem to have anything to do with each other.". . . If the reader is brought to accept both the effects in question and the explanation he will have helped validate what is, in essence, a theory of reading.

(Culler 1981: 113).

However, as postmodern novels themselves affirm, meaning is irrevocably ambiguous and plural. There is no longer even the pretense that reality can be directly mirrored by a novel, although several of them take great delight in playing with this notion. Reality is a purely linguistic construct and, if any mirroring takes place, it is of linguistic structures: "all literary texts are woven out of other literary texts, not in the conventional sense that they bear the traces of 'influence' but in the more radical sense that every word, phrase or segment is a reworking of other writings which precede or surround the individual work. There is no such thing as literary 'originality', no such thing as the 'first' literary work: all literature is intertextual" (Eagleton 1983: 138). This is a literary development of Saussure's theory of difference. If "language is a system of interdependent terms in which the value of each term results solely from the simultaneous presence of the others" (Saussure 1915: 114), then the same can be said of the literature that is created by that language. This is the guiding principle behind Roland Barthes' essay "The Death of the Author" in which he argues for a shift of critical emphasis from author to reader precisely because it is "language which speaks, not the author; to write is, through a prerequisite impersonality (not at all to be confused with the castrating objectivity of the realist novelist), to reach that point where only language acts, 'performs,' and not 'me'" (1977: 143). This essay combines elements of, and is therefore a good bridge between, "high" structuralist and post-structuralist theories of text and reader. Primarily, Barthes argues from the structuralist position that reality is a linguistic construct. Similarly, then, language recog-nizes the authorial "I" or "me" *only* as a linguistic subject, not as a person with passions, humours, or feelings which exist anterior to the text (Barthes 1977: 145). What is anterior to the text, however, is both language itself and other texts, and for this reason the author's subjectivity is only a "ready-formed dictionary, its words only explainable through other words, and so on indefinitely" (ibid.: 146). Authority is limiting, Barthes argues, because to impose an "Author" is to impose a single, fixed meaning. Since postmodern texts stress their multiplicity of meaning because of the plurality inherent in language, the structure of the text should be "*disentangled*" instead of simply "*deciphered*" (Barthes 1977: 147). The focus of this activity is the reader because it is between reader and text that the "mutual relations of dialogue, parody, contestation" (ibid.: 148) take place.

Barthes' view of language not simply as a system of difference, but as a "systematic exemption of meaning" (1977: 147) which "ceaselessly calls into question all origins" (ibid.: 146), moves toward the extreme relativism of post-structuralist, and in particular deconstructionist theories. Structuralism sees texts as composed of binary oppositions (such as good/bad, light/dark, male/female). According to theories of deconstruction, however, these antitheses create ideological problems because their own structure privileges one term (usually the first) over another, and because this opposition is not an end in itself, but a hierarchy which can be further deconstructed. Binarism presupposes an absolute, and it is this authoritarianism that deconstruction tries to subvert. As Jacques Derrida explains in *Positions*:

> In a classical philosophical opposition we are not dealing with the peaceful coexistence of *vis-à-vis*, but rather with a violent hierarchy. One of the two terms governs the other (axio-logically, logically, etc.), or has the upper hand. To decon-struct the opposition, first of all, is to overturn the hierarchy at a given moment. To overlook this phase of overturning is to forget the conflictual and subordinating structure of opposition.
> (Derrida 1981: 41)

Structuralist difference, he argues, assumes that there is a value in opposition that precedes that opposition:

> At the point at which the concept of *différance*, and the chain attached to it, intervenes, all the conceptual oppositions of metaphysics (signifier/signified; sensible/intelligible; writing/speech; passivity/activity; etc.) – to the extent that they ultimately refer to the presence of something present (for example, in the form of the identity of the subject who is

present for all his operations, present beneath every accident of event, self-present in its "living speech," in its enunciations, in the present objects and acts of its language, etc.) – become nonpertinent. They all amount, at one moment or another, to a subordination of the movement of *différance* in favour of the presence of a value or a *meaning* supposedly antecedent to *différance*, more original than it, exceeding and governing it in the last analysis. This is still the presence of what we called above the "transcendental signified."

(Derrida 1981: 29)

For deconstruction, then, as for structuralism, the text is plural. However, here it is infinitely plural and irreducible to any rigidly defined opposition. Every text – theoretical, critical, biographical, or historical – will ultimately subvert its rhetorical strategies. To deconstruct a text or discourse is to show how it undermines the "philosophy it asserts, or the hierarchical oppositions on which it relies, by identifying in the text the rhetorical operations that produce the supposed grounds of argument, the key concept or premise" (Culler 1982: 86).

These recent linguistic and critical theories are, in every sense, attacks on Realism and its attendant ideology of liberal humanism, and as such have been seen by traditionalists as everything from problematic to the end of Culture and Civilization.[5] This is particularly because they attack the Realist view that each text has a magically inscribed, single truth which is the reflection of a moral mind, and which can be extracted by means of common sense (see Belsey 1980: 1–36). Much criticism today, however, denies that language is neutral and natural, and insists, as a correlative of this, that criticism itself is ideological. Critics such as Catherine Belsey, Terry Eagleton, and Edward Said see Realism as a tool of ideological control, precisely *because* it pretends to be normal and neutral. To argue, then, that the world and our experience of it are discontinuous with one another is a threat because it questions the very nature of "reality" and "truth" (Eagleton 1983: 108). The theory which claims that these are merely linguistic constructs with no absolute value radically undermines a whole system of social and pedagogical control which depends for its power on there being a "good" or a "truth" which is transcendental. Postmodern texts are both the inheritors and the perpetrators of this radical undermining. Like linguistic theorists, they posit a straw man of Realism, while at the same time, they unravel the fabric of their own language through the discourses of history, performance, visual art, and film.

Chapter two

Telling li(v)es
History and historiographic
metafiction

The quarrels of popes and kings, with wars or pestilences, in every page; the men all so good for nothing, and hardly any women at all – it is very tiresome: and yet I often think it odd that it should be so dull, for a great deal of it must be invention. The speeches that are put into the heroes' mouths, their thoughts and designs – the chief of all this must be invention, and invention is what delights me in other books.

Jane Austen, *Northanger Abbey* 1972: 123

As has been discussed, the Realist aesthetic tended to distinguish between "lying" literature and "true," "objective" history, and to ascribe a positive moral value to fact. History was seen as accessible as pure fact, independent of individual perception, ideology, or the process of selection necessitated simply by creating a written narrative. As historian Hayden White points out in "The Fictions of Factual Representation," this "empiricist prejudice" was attended by the conviction that " 'reality' is not only perceivable but is also coherent in its structure" (1976: 22). This notion of coherence, however, is perhaps why the Realists praised Sir Walter Scott's historical novels as appearing to exemplify their literary principles. In 1825, in *The Spirit of the Age*, William Hazlitt described Scott as a " *'prophesier'* of things past" (1969: 96), and an "amanuensis of truth and history" (ibid.: 104):

Sir Walter Scott has found out (O rare discovery) that facts are better than fiction, that there is no romance like the romance of real life, and that, if we can but arrive at what men feel, do, and say in striking and singular situations, the result will be "more lively, audible, and full of vent," than the fine-spun cobwebs of the brain. . . . Our author has conjured up the actual people he has to deal with, or as much as he could get of them, in "their habits as they lived." He has ransacked old chronicles, and poured the contents upon his page; he has squeezed out musty records; he has consulted wayfaring pilgrims, bed-rid sybils. He has invoked the spirits of the air; he has conversed with the living and the dead, and let them tell their story their own way; and by borrowing of others has enriched his own genius with everlasting variety, truth, and freedom. He has taken his materials from the original, authentic sources in large concrete masses, and not tampered with or too much frittered them away.

(Hazlitt 1969: 103–4)

The combination of fiction and history, particularly in Scott's novels, seemed to fulfil the Realist demands for objectivity, detail, democracy, and, above all, factual documentation. Henry James, for example, in "Fiction and Sir Walter Scott," praises Scott's novels as the "triumphs of fact" (1864: 587). The historical novel also allayed many of the Realist's fears about the immoral influence of fiction. Edward Bulwer-Lytton, himself an historical novelist, explains this in didactic, Aristotelian terms in his essay on historical romance: "The historical event is referred to for the purpose of giving consistency and probability to the plot, and the persons are introduced as the landmarks whereof the manners are representative. Opportunity is thus afforded to instruct as well as to amuse" (1970: 330). Scott's credentials for taking on this function of instructor appear to have been excellent. Aside from his fictional works, he wrote or edited numerous historical texts. Yet it was his fiction that Thomas Carlyle (not, as we have seen, an avowed admirer of the genre) praised for vitalizing history in "Sir Walter Scott":

These Historical novels have taught all men this truth, which looks like a truism, and yet was as good as unknown to writers of history and others, till so taught: that the bygone ages of the world were actually filled by living men not by protocols, state-papers, controversies and abstractions of men. Not abstractions were they, not diagrams and theorems; but men in buff or other coats or breeches, with colour in their cheeks with passions in their stomach, and the idioms, features and vitalities of very men. It is a little word this; inclusive of great meaning! History will henceforth have to take thought of it. Her faint hearsays of "philosophy teaching by experience" will have to exchange themselves everywhere for direct inspection and embodiment: this, and this only, will be counted experience; and till once experience has got in, philosophy will reconcile herself to wait at the door. It is a great service, fertile in consequences that this Scott has done; a great truth laid open by him: – correspondent indeed to the substantial nature of the man; to his solidity and veracity even of imagination, which with all his lively discursiveness was the characteristic of him.

(Carlyle 1899: vol. 4: 77–8)

Not all of Scott's critics, however, were as lavish in their praise. For some, the combination of fiction and history was problematic. An anonymous reviewer of *Quentin Durward* in *New Monthly Magazine* criticizes Scott for taking liberty with historical fact. While the reviewer allows that the historical novelist "may omit facts, or add to them inventions which are in keeping with what is known," he is not at liberty to "distort the truth by a transfer of events and personages, by which, under the disguise of amusement, he gives false impressions, unsettles men's notions, and renders in great degree nugatory, one of the most laborious and useful of human studies" (Hayden 1970: 278). Another anonymous reviewer of *Ivanhoe* in *Eclectic Review* simply dislikes "that mongrel sort of production, an historical novel" (Hayden 1970: 193), because in the combination of history and romance, "the illusion is never complete: the grand facts of history are perpetually forcing themselves upon the recollection in all their unromantic truth and moral importance, while a competitor interest to which the imagination is quite disposed to yield, is ever soliciting the feelings, and awakening emotions of an opposite nature" (ibid.: 191).

Walter Scott himself was not insensitive to the criticisms of this new genre. Since his novels were published anonymously, he addresses the problems in prefaces or dedicatory letters to his novels. In both the "Dedicatory Epistle" to *Ivanhoe*, and the "Prefatory Letter" to *Peveril of the Peak* he answers the charges of "the severer antiquary" that by "thus intermingling fiction with truth, [he is] polluting the well of history with modern inventions" (Scott 1819: xlvi–xlvii), and that by the same process he is "adulterating the pure sources of historical knowledge" (Scott, 1823: lxxiv). It is interesting that the "Author," in his defense against these criticisms, is much less concerned with the historical truth of his novels than are either his defenders or detractors. The purpose of the "Author", he tells us in *Peveril*, is to impart through his historical tales, "a degree of knowledge, not perhaps of the most accurate kind," but such as the reader "might not otherwise have acquired" (Scott 1823: lxxvii). In order to excite this knowledge, he suggests in *Ivanhoe* that the historical subject should be "translated into the manners, as well as the language, of the age we live in" (Scott 1819: xlvii). To do this in such a way that the reader is not "trammelled by the repulsive dryness of antiquity" (ibid.: xlviii), it is necessary to fictionalize rather than mirror events of the past. The "Author" in *Peveril of the Peak* stresses the creativity of his reconstruction of history:

A poor fellow, like myself, weary with ransacking his own barren and bounded imagination, looks out for some general subject in the huge and boundless field of history, which holds forth examples of every kind – lights on some personage or some combination of circumstances, or some striking trait of manners, which he thinks may be advantageously used as the basis of a fictitious narrative – bedizens it with such colouring as his skill suggests – ornaments it with such romantic circumstances as may heighten the general effect – invests it with such shades of character, as will best contrast with each other – and thinks, perhaps, he has done some service to the public, if he can present to them a lively fictitious picture, for which the original anecdote or circumstance which he made free to press into his service, only furnished a slight sketch. Now I cannot perceive any harm in this. The stores of history are accessible to every one; and are no more exhausted or impoverished by the hints thus borrowed from them than the fountain is drained by the water which we subtract for domestic purposes. And in reply to the sober charge of falsehood, against a narrative announced positively to be fictitious, one can only answer, by

Prior's exclamation, "Odzooks, must one swear to the truth of a song?"

(Scott 1823: lxxv)

The historical romance as a genre creates levels of illusion and "reality," and Scott reinforces these levels through his use of historiographic and literary devices. In fact, his literal anonymity prompted readers and critics alike to imitate the creative process Scott outlines above. The "Author of *Waverley*" became a figure for "fictional" speculation, and even after his identity was generally agreed upon, his motives continued to be topics for discussion. More conventional literary devices designed to give the illusion of "reality" include the framing of one story within another (*The Heart of Midlothian*), a fictional editor (*Peveril of the Peak* among others), and, in several of the novels, end-notes which, although they give details of the "real" historical events in the fictions, serve mainly to highlight the fictiveness of those events as they appear in the novels. Scott's choice of titles also enforces the various levels of fiction and "reality." The title, *The Heart of Midlothian*, for example, refers to the historical Edinburgh tolbooth, a prison which is also fictionalized in the novel. Yet the description of the prison within the novel is also an appropriate description of the novel as, to use Frederic Jameson's phrase, a "prison-house of language," and it gives the novel the same ontological status as the historical tolbooth:

> a prison is a world within itself, and has its own business, griefs and joys, peculiar to its circle. Its inmates are sometimes short-lived, but so are soldiers on service; they are poor relatively to the world without, but there are degrees of wealth and poverty among them, and so some are relatively rich also. They cannot stir abroad, but neither can the garrison of a besieged fort, or the crew of a ship at sea; and they are not under a dispensation quite so desperate as either, for they may have as much food as they have money to buy, and are not obliged to work whether they have food or not.

(Scott 1818: 13)

Scott, then, can be seen to use history in a slightly different way than that for which the Realists praised him. However, as is evident from the quotation above, he stresses the mimetic quality of his fiction. He certainly agrees with the Realist idea of history as "pure," universally accessible through manuscripts and other documents, and, above all, as educational. What this points to about the Realists, however, is just how limiting their conventions were. *The Heart of Midlothian* as a novel is certainly conscious of the multiplicity of language, yet on the level of *theory* especially, this is something the Realists ignored, focusing instead on how well their dictates were fulfilled.

As was pointed out in the previous chapter, linguistic theorists have questioned our ability to perceive the world as unmediated by language. From this perspective, is it possible to believe, as the Realists did, that we can apprehend history as a synthetic, self-structured body of pure, non-linguistic fact? Equally, how can fiction and history really be antithetical, if both are realized in language? In "The Fictions of Factual Representation," Hayden White addresses these issues from the point of view of an historian. He argues that the nineteenth-century opposition of fiction and history arose in response to the "mythic" thinking which, it was believed, had led to the "excesses and failures of the [French] Revolution" (White 1976: 25):

> It became imperative to rise above any impulses to interpret the historical record in the light of party prejudices, utopian expectations, or sentimental attachments to traditional institutions. In order to find one's way among the conflicting claims of the parties which took shape during and after the Revolution, it was necessary to locate some standpoint of social perception that was truly "objective," truly "realistic."
> (White 1976: 26)

The aim, then, of historical discourse became to produce "factually accurate statements about a realm of events which were (or had been) observable in principle, the arrangement of which in the order of their true original occurrence would permit them to figure forth their true meaning or significance" (ibid.: 25). White argues in this, as in other essays, and most notably in his book *Metahistory*, that the way in which we know the past is through historiography which is subject to the same creative processes as fiction. The writing of history, as he points out, in "The Fictions of Factual Representation," is a "poetic process" (White 1976: 28). In "The Historical Text as Literary Artifact" he argues that historical narratives are "verbal fictions, the contents of which are as much invented as found and the forms of which have more in common with their counterparts in literature than they have with those in the sciences" (1978: 42). White places historiography on the same plane as fiction, but denigrates neither. As he sees it, both use conventional literary structures – tragedy, comedy, irony, metaphor, among others – in order to manipulate the reader's perception:

> Historical situations are not inherently tragic, comic, or romantic. They may all be inherently ironic, but they need not be emplotted that way. All the historian needs to do to transform a tragic into a comic situation is to shift his point of view or change the scope of his perceptions. In any case, we only think of situations as tragic or comic because these concepts are part of our generally cultural and specifically literary heritage. How a given historical situation is to be configured depends on the historian's subtlety in matching a specific plot-structure with the set of historical events that he wishes to endow with a meaning of a particular kind. This is essentially a literary, that is to say fiction-making aspiration.
>
> (White 1978: 49)

Clearly, the idea of history as discursive practice is informed by the linguistic theories which challenge the traditional position that language is transparent, that the word is the direct means to the thing it represents, and that the connection between them is natural and ideologically neutral. This challenge is apparent, not just in linguistic and theoretical writings, but in the postmodern novels which use history as both a reference to the "real" past world, *and* as a text or discursive construct (Hutcheon 1984: xiv). This differs substantially from the use of history in the traditional historical novel where history, as a group of facts which exists extra-textually and which can be represented as it "really was," is never in question. While the skeleton of factual information is filled in with fictional flesh in order to make it more presentable, there is never any doubt as to the factual or structural make-up of the skeleton. The very form of these novels borrows from traditional narrative history in its linearity, examination of cause and effect, and emphasis on the primacy of the individual subject.

In recent metafictional texts which deal with history, such Realist issues appear to be of equal importance. These novels create an illusion of "reality" by representing people, places, and events which are historically verifiable (for example: Gustave Flaubert in *Flaubert's Parrot*; Nicholas Hawksmoor's six London churches in *Hawksmoor*; the Indian language riots in *Midnight's Children*). The use of "real" names, places, and events however, is asserted and almost immediately rendered problematic. Some of these novels borrow from the nineteenth-century tradition of displacement, in that they appear to present themselves not as novels, but as biography (*Flaubert's Parrot*), autobiography (*Midnight's Children*), memoir (*Waterland*), and, above all, as documentary history.

The novels cited above are what Linda Hutcheon, in *Narcissistic Narrative*, calls "historiographic metafictions" (1984: xiv), and they are, particularly in their play with Realist conventions, paradoxical. While they use Realist conventions, they simultaneously seek to subvert them. Yet they do so from within precisely those conventions which they are clearly trying to undermine. Like all metafictional texts, historiographic metafiction puts the reader in a contradictory position. As Hutcheon explains:

> On the one hand, he is forced to acknowledge the artifice, the "art," of what he is reading; on the other, explicit demands are made upon him, as co-creator, for intellectual and affective responses comparable in scope and intensity to those of his life experience. In fact, these responses are shown to be *part of* his life experience. In this light metafiction is less a departure from the mimetic novelistic tradition than a reworking of it.
>
> (Hutcheon 1984: 5)

In historiographic metafiction, this problem is further complicated. Since the novels present themselves as documentary history *and* as artifice, the reader must come to terms with the referential and non-referential nature of the literature at the same time. While he or she recognizes that the historically verifiable events, people, and places exist(ed), he or she must also recognize them, in Hayden White's terms, as discourse. The problems for the reader of historiographic metafiction can be clearly seen in *Flaubert's Parrot*, *Midnight's Children*, and *Waterland*, novels in which the question of *how* we know history is thematized.

In *Flaubert's Parrot* by Julian Barnes, Geoffrey Braithwaite appears initially to be a clearly Realist reader whose search for direct correspondence between fiction and reality is nevertheless subverted by the very structure of the text of which he is the narrator. In his eyes, Flaubert's novels are the key to Flaubert, and Flaubert, who proved himself in *Madame Bovary* to be the master of creative adultery, is the key to unlocking the mysteries of his own troubles with the wandering affections of his wife. In trying to sort out his own problems, he tries to reconstruct Flaubert's world as Flaubert might have seen it:

> So Gustave was a six-foot giant, and the world shrinks just a little with that knowledge. The giants were not so tall (were the dwarves therefore shorter too?). The fat men: were they less fat because they were smaller, and so you needed less stomach to appear fat; or were they more fat because they developed the same stomachs, but had less frame to support them? How can we know such trivial, crucial details? We can study files for decades, but every so often we are tempted to throw up our hands and declare that history is just another literary genre: the past is autobiographical fiction pretending to be a parliamentary report.
>
> (Barnes 1984: 90)

Despite his occasional frustration that history will not yield itself up to him as an uncomplicated whole, Braithwaite persists in his determined search. He is not, however, naive enough to overlook the contradictions inherent in his quest, particularly since Flaubert "disdainfully forbade posterity to take any personal interest in him" (Barnes 1984: 16). Nevertheless, he toils after the truth even while he questions his own motives and comments on how easily history can be counterfeited:

> What makes us randy for relics? Don't we believe the words enough? Do we think the leavings of a life contain some ancillary truth? When Robert Louis Stevenson died, his business-minded Scottish nanny quietly began selling hair which she claimed to have cut from the writer's head forty years earlier. The believers, the seekers, the pursuers bought enough of it to stuff a sofa.
>
> (Barnes 1984: 12)

Armed as he is with such examples, Braithwaite nevertheless

37

visits Rouen, Croisset, and two collections of Flaubert memorabilia, at each of which he finds the supposedly authentic stuffed parrot which was Flaubert's model for Loulou in *Un coeur simple*. Flaubert, according to the letters which Braithwaite quotes, did indeed borrow a stuffed parrot from the Rouen Museum of Natural History, and this ghost of a "real" referent gives Braithwaite hope of establishing a tangible link with the writer. To this end, he writes letters to academics, the French Embassy, the editor of the Michelin guide-books, and David Hockney on the strength of his illustration for *Un coeur simple, Félicité Sleeping with a Parrot*, hoping for authentication of one of the birds. He also examines possible resemblances between the writer and his story: "Félicité + Loulou = Flaubert? Not exactly; but you could claim that he is present in both of them. Félicité encloses his character; Loulou encloses his voice" (Barnes 1984: 18), and carefully charts the "four principal encounters between the novelist and a member of the parrot family" (ibid.: 18). Even with a copy of *Un coeur simple* in hand, Braithwaite cannot be sure that either parrot matches Flaubert's description. Finally, he visits a Flaubert scholar, and yet the story he is told in response to his question does not solve the mystery. The two commemorative museums, at their inceptions, sent their curators to retrieve the parrot Flaubert borrowed from the Museum of Natural History. Although the two Flaubert collections were founded forty years apart, their curators had the same shock:

> They opened the door, and they saw in front of them. . . fifty parrots. *Une cinquantaine de perroquets*! What did they do? They did the logical thing, the intelligent thing. They came back with a copy of *Un coeur simple*, and they read to themselves Flaubert's description of Loulou. . . . And then they chose the parrot which looked most like his description.
>
> (Barnes 1984: 187)

The revelation that the "real" stuffed parrot might have been given away, might have rotted away, or might simply have been authorial invention both pleases and disappoints Braithwaite. His contradictory reaction is an appropriate one however, since, while as a character Braithwaite is obsessed by concerns we might associate with Realist reading – detail, authority, intention, reference – as a narrator, he constantly undermines his own obsessions. In this role he is self-conscious and intrusive. He offers the reader advice on cheese, dictates types of novels which should and should not be written, "There is to be a twenty-year ban on novels set in Oxford or Cambridge, and a ten-year ban on other university fiction. No ban on fiction set in polytechnics (though no subsidy to encourage it)" (Barnes 1984: 98–9), and forbids the reader to pursue him ("Besides, I'm going to the lavatory first. I can't have you following me in there, peering round from the next stall" (ibid.: 90). He offers parodic imitations of Flaubert's *Dictionnaire des idées reçues*, of chronologies of Flaubert's life, a version of their relationship from the point of view of Louise Colet, and even an examination paper.

Each of these is, to some extent, a parrot, a way of imitating Flaubert in the hope that the imitation will reflect the truth. Conversely, that such multiple ways of seeing exist provides an acknowledgement that there is no single truth any more than there is a single parrot. The parrot becomes, in fact, a symbol for the novel's play with conflicting views of the function of literature. A parrot can do no more than reflect external reality. This is what Braithwaite hopes for in seeking the model for Loulou, whose very name gives credence to his quest. Having found it, he thinks, he will have found the writer. However, a crucial conflict arises here. Flaubert's parrot is, perhaps, a tangible, actual object. Braithwaite tries to prove as much by quoting the documentary evidence of Flaubert's letters.

Both the story and the letters, however, are linguistic constructs which exist in *Flaubert's Parrot*, itself a fiction. Gustave Flaubert is an historically verifiable entity, but we can only know him through the written evidence of novels, letters, and reminiscences. As the narrative shows, there is no single, direct correspondence between the written word and "reality." Language creates "reality," and language is inescapably plural. It is not surprising, then, that Braithwaite should discover that a parrot is not only a bird but a type of soup: "bread dipped in rough red wine" (Barnes 1984: 84); a house with a single room on each story: "The French call such a house *un bâton de perroquet*, a parrot's perch" (ibid.: 107); and a restaurant: "It was called Le Perroquet. Outside, on the pavement, a fretworked wooden parrot with garish green plumage was holding the lunch menu in its beak" (ibid.: 112). As a narrator, he cannot but create an indeterminate Flaubert, Flaubert's parrot, and *Flaubert's Parrot*.

The reader of historiographic metafiction is in a similarly contradictory position. On the one hand, these novels maintain that there is a "parrot," an historical subject which can somehow be traced and which, when found, will be found whole. On the other, they are irrevocably self-conscious, asserting through structure and conflicting information that the "parrot" is a discursive construct.

Like Geoffrey Braithwaite, Tom Crick, the narrator of Graham Swift's *Waterland*, looks to the past to explain, and assuage his fear of, the present. His wife has been placed in an asylum after having kidnapped a baby, he is about to lose his job as a high school history teacher because, as his headmaster tells him, "We're cutting back history" (Swift 1983: 18), and his students are in revolt at having to study the French Revolution which, they protest, has no relevance to the "here and now" (ibid.: 6). Their complaint stems from their "collective night-mares" (ibid.: 6) of nuclear war: "The only important thing about history, I think, sir, is that it's got to the point where it's probably about to end" (ibid.: 6). To quell the fears of his young students, Crick resorts to a different kind of fairy-tale from that of the French Revolution:

> Children, who will inherit the world. Children to whom, throughout history, stories have been told, chiefly but not always at bedtime, in order to quell restless thoughts; whose need of stories is matched only by the need adults have of children to tell stories to, of receptacles for their stock of fairy-tales, of listening ears on which to unload, bequeath those most unbelievable yet haunting of fairy-tales, their own lives.
>
> (Swift 1983: 6)

History becomes, therefore, *his* story, told to his students as part fact, part make-believe.

That "story" is literally contained in "history" is clear from the first epigraph where *historia* is defined by and as narrative: "*Historia*, ae, f.1. inquiry, investigation, learning. 2. a) a narrative of past events, history. b) any kind of narrative: account, tale, story" (Swift 1983: ix). One of Crick's constant concerns and frustrations is with the definition of history, which turns out to be as various as the above list suggests. It is at once the "Grand Narrative" (Swift 1983.: 53), "fairy-tale" (ibid.: 6), a teacher of "reality" (ibid.: 94), the search for "cause and effect" (ibid.: 92), a way of ascertaining the truth (ibid.: 227), and fact (ibid.: 74). Above all, however, it is uncertainty: "history is that impossible thing: the attempt to give an account, with incomplete knowledge, of actions themselves undertaken with incomplete knowledge" (Swift 1983.: 94). It is interesting, then, that the first epigraph should be a dictionary definition since it, too, has a contradictory status. The dictionary is usually used as an authoritative repository of meaning, but it is also the ultimate self-referential text. Even the most casual glance at the *Oxford English Dictionary* confirms that language is indefinite, that meaning is a construction as indeed is language.

As if to emphasize this point, the second epigraph is from an overtly fictional text, Charles Dickens' *Great Expectations*: "'Ours was the marsh country . . .'" (Swift 1983: ix). Here, too, there is an appeal to authority, but it is the authority of *both* the "real" past (*Great Expectations* as a tangible object) and of fiction. *Great Expectations* is clearly an intertext in *Waterland*, and there are several points of comparison. Both begin and end in marsh country. Pip tries to escape his own past in the same way as Price tries to escape history, and in both novels there is the double narrative perspective of an adult examining his childhood; lost expectations lead both narrators to revisit or re-examine the past. Once there, however, they react in different ways. Pip learns from history. There is a clearly didactic formula imposed on the past which is primarily one of cause and effect. Pip sees the error of his ways and tries to repair them.

Tom Crick, however, even though he is a history teacher, is concerned less with the didacticism of history than he is with the ways in which history can be structured as narrative. One of the tensions in the novel between past and future is, in fact, alluded to in the epigraph's play with tense: "'Ours *was* the marsh country. . . .'" Crick describes history in a way which also describes the novel: "It goes in two directions at once. It goes backwards as it goes forwards. It loops. It takes detours. Do not fall into the illusion that history is a well disciplined and unflagging column marching unswervingly into the future" (Swift 1983: 117). He calls his adolescent self a "future history teacher" (ibid.: 101), and while what he is narrating is his past, it is simultaneously the future which will unfold for the reader. It is so cleverly structured that the end of the novel is only mid way through the story. We know by the end of the novel that what happens after the final chapter is contained in the first few chapters which means, if we read circuitously, going back to the past.

Unlike many metafictional texts, however, *Waterland* does not at first appear to foreground its structure. It presents itself as what Roland Barthes calls in *S/Z*, a *lisible* (readable) text rather than a *scriptible* (writable) text (1975: 4). The story is so engaging and the manipulation of affect so intense that it can certainly be read (if naively) on this level. However, the *process* of making/imposing meanings on historical events is one of Crick's obsessions: "the more you try to dissect events, the more you lose hold of what you took for granted in the first place – the more it seems it never actually occurred, but occurs, somehow, only in the imagination" (Swift 1983: 121); "History: a lucky dip of meanings. Events elude meaning, but we look for meanings. Another definition of Man: the animal who craves meaning – but knows" (ibid.: 122). Crick, then, tries to decide just what history is and how to present it. The multiple ways in which he structures his narrative make it clear that "a good story" is just one of the ploys he uses in his attempt to impose meaning. After all, the other "definition of Man" he refers to above is as "the story-telling animal" (ibid.: 53).

The novel as a whole plays with the notion that history is circular. Not only does the end direct us back to the beginning, but events recur throughout, featuring different actors. This point is stressed by the novel's fifty-two chapters, as well as by Crick's dog which is, appropriately enough, a retriever. It is clear, however, that the narrator's choice of language and form is responsible for the circularity in a way that the events themselves could not be. In the following quotation, he synthesizes events in such a way that history itself does indeed seem to repeat and foreshadow itself:

> But meanwhile that scene on the Lode bank which, like other scenes yet to come, lodges in your history teacher's memory to be exhumed at later dates. Mary in navy blue knickers which she has shared briefly with an eel; a live fish in a woman's lap;

Dick; Freddie Parr; their stares, with his own, forming an
invisible cat's cradle. A bottle hurled into the muddy Lode;
Dick on the wooden bridge; Freddie in the water. . . . Now
who says history doesn't go in circles?

(Swift 1983: 180)

Frequent references to the French Revolution – Crick draws
parallels between this and his personal history – however, point
out that while circularity is one possible way to interpret history,
yet another, equally appropriate one, might be that history
"undergoes periodic convulsions" (Swift 1983: 119), is a series of
ruptures: the very word "revolution" includes the possibility of
both a return to and a break from the past:

Children, do you remember when we did the French
Revolution? That great landmark, that great watershed of
history. How I explained to you the implications of that word
"revolution"? A turning round, a completing of a cycle. How I
told you that though the popular notion of a revolution is that
of categorical change transformation – a progressive leap into
the future – yet almost every revolution contains within it an
opposite if less obvious tendency: the idea of a return. A
redemption; a restoration. A reaffirmation of what is pure and
fundamental against what is decadent and false. A return to a
new beginning. . . .

(Swift 1983: 119)

Just as the structure of *Waterland* suggests a circular reading of
both the novel and of history, so does it, paradoxically, suggest
reading for rupture. Some chapter breaks mark moments of
change from past to present or present to past. Yet what they
point to is not return, but discontinuity. This is especially so in
that the aleatory movement of the novel parallels the erratic
pattern of memory.

Two further structures that Crick imposes on history and his
story are the linear and archaeological. The repetition of details –
bottles, beer, eels, fire, rivers – makes history (and story) seem as
though it is moving forward, building on itself, and giving us
recognizable signposts with which to chart its progress. For
example, some chapters are grammatically continuous. At the
end of Chapter two, Crick leads into the next chapter without

punctuation: "And since a fairy-tale must have a setting, a setting which, like the setting of all good fairy-tales, must be both palpable and unreal, let me tell you. . . . About the Fens [title of Chapter three] Which are a low-lying region . . . [beginning of Chapter three]" (Swift 1983: 6–7). A final method Crick uses to make sense of the past is what Michel Foucault has called "archaeological." Crick takes various of the items in the world around him and examines *their* history. This takes part in both the linear – these mini-histories are structured chronologically – and discontinuous – his forays into natural history, scientific discoveries, genealogies, interrupt the personal history he is trying to narrate – modes of meaning production.

Clearly, meaning and structure are imposed on history by narrative devices. Memory, too, plays a large part here, not just because it magnifies and effaces "real" events, but because it *creates* its own "truth." This is clear in *Waterland* from two "mistakes" that the narrator makes which show us the very process of re-creating the past. When Thomas Atkinson, Crick's great, great-grandfather dies, his funeral takes place on a day about which Crick says:

> History does not record whether the day of Thomas's funeral was one of those dazzling mid-winter Fenland days in which the sky seems to cleanse every outline and make light of distances and the two towers of Ely cathedral can not only be seen but their contrasting architecture plainly described. . . . But such things would have been appropriate.
>
> (Swift 1983: 70–1)

Several pages later, the weather is no longer a matter for speculation: "compare the unbefitting sunshine of old Tom's funeral day" (ibid.: 84). When Freddie Parr's body is found floating in his father's lock, Crick, as a young boy, is shocked because "I realised I was looking at a dead body. Something I had never seen before. (For I had seen mother dying but not dead)" (Swift 1983: 25). Later, when he describes his mother's death, however, he says: "For when, after making that fateful if ill-judged announcement, [that their mother is dead] Dad led us both across the upstairs passage – because he wouldn't deny or spare us this final privilege – to take our last look at Mother" (ibid.: 245). These two incidents are clear examples that narrating *makes* things real. There is no way to know "facts" outside the telling/writing of them.

In the course of his narrative, Tom Crick emphasizes the Fenlanders' love of story-telling in which fact and superstition have only fluid boundaries. They spin yarns in order to give shape to the "wide, empty space" (Swift 1983: 15) of the landscape, to fill in gaps in available knowledge, and to provide explanations for what cannot otherwise be explained. As a boy, Crick

> piously observed, because others observed them too, a catechism of obscure rites. When you see the new moon, turn your money in your pocket; help someone to salt and help them to sorrow; never put new shoes on a table or cut your nails on a Sunday. An eel-skin cures rheumatism; a roast mouse cures whooping cough; and a live fish in a woman's lap will make her barren.
>
> (Swift 1983: 15–16)

Story-telling provides the link between public and private history since, while all historical events are direct experience to *someone*, to everyone else, they are simply stories. The "echoes from the wide world" (Swift 1983: 16) that reach the Fens, then, are as "real" or as fictional to the Fenlanders as are their superstitions. Having heard of the rebellion of the colonies, Waterloo, or the Crimea, "they listened and repeated what they heard with wide-eyed awe, as if such things were not the stuff of fact but the fabric of a wondrous tale" (ibid. 16). Not surprisingly, the threads of history and superstition also intertwine in Crick's explanation of more domestic events. His wife Mary is barren because, when pregnant as a teenager, she attempts to induce a miscarriage which results in a crude abortion performed by the local "witch," Martha Clay. This scene is graphically described as the "real" reason behind Mary's inability to have children. Equally important, however, is that when Mary was a teenager, Freddie Parr dropped a live eel into her "school regulation knickers" (Swift 1983: 167) and, as Crick repeats twice, "a live fish in a woman's lap will make her barren" (ibid.: 16, 180). Clearly *both* reasons are necessary to Crick to explain Mary's history, and both are constructions, because narrated.

Both *Flaubert's Parrot* and *Waterland* thematize the contradictory nature of historiographic metafiction. On one hand, they assure the reader of the certainty of historical events, yet on the other, they point to the indeterminacy of such events because of how we come to know them. Both refer to recognizably "real" entities: Flaubert, the French Revolution, Christopher Ricks, London, Rouen, etc. However, neither novel deals with the problem of a fictional character, who, in the course of the novel, participates in historical events or interacts with historical personages in order to highlight one of the most tenacious of realist doctrines: the binary opposition of fact and fiction. The Fenlanders absorb both fictive and factual discourse: stories fill the empty space of "reality," and "reality" becomes the stuff of stories. *Flaubert's Parrot*, however, raises the issue of what role factual information plays in fictional discourse. Braithwaite agrees with "Christopher Ricks" in his lecture on "Mistakes in Literature and Whether They Matter," whose theme is "that if the factual side of literature becomes unreliable, then ploys such as irony and fantasy become much harder to use. If you don't know what's true or what's meant to be true, then the value of what isn't true or what isn't meant to be true becomes diminished" (Barnes 1984: 77). In "Ricks'" terms, then, the literariness of the text can only be recognized in opposition to the factual, and the factual would seem to be seen here as extra-textual. The presence of factual or documentary information in metafictional texts often seems to validate fictional events, as it does in Scott's novels. In John Fowles' *The French Lieutenant's Woman*, for example, Charles works in the same library as does Karl Marx, and Sarah Woodruff lives with the Rossettis. Similarly, in Timothy Findley's *Famous Last Words*, Hugh Selwyn Mauberley meets Ezra Pound as well as the Duke and Duchess of Windsor. These fictional characters, then, are given the same ontological status as the "real" characters. Equally, however, the "real" characters who exist or existed are fictionalized: they both are and are not the entities who are designated by their names. Their ontology, thus, is called into question, as it is even more radically in *Midnight's Children* by Salman Rushdie.

In "Historical Discourse," Roland Barthes argues that "the only feature which distinguishes historical discourse from other kinds is a paradox: the 'fact' can exist linguistically only as a term in a discourse, yet we behave as if it were a simple reproduction of something on another plane of existence altogether, some extra-structural 'reality.' Historical discourse is presumably the only kind which can aim at a referent 'outside' itself that can in fact never be reached" (1970: 153). But, the same can be said of the historical discourse in historiographic metafiction. In *Midnight's Children*, as in *Waterland*, historical events and people are combined with magic and fantasy. These latter elements, it is suggested, appear to be the only ways to approach an understanding of an incomprehensible "reality." The narrator, Saleem Sinai, is born on the stroke of midnight August 15, 1947, the moment of India's independence from British rule. As such, he (like the other children born in the first hour of the new country) is the child "*of the time*: fathered, you understand, by history" (Rushdie 1981: 118). A letter from Jawaharlal Nehru, congratulating him on the accident of his birth at such an auspicious moment, encourages Saleem to see himself as an integral part of India's history: "You are the newest bearer of that ancient face of India which is also eternally young. We shall be watching over your life with the closest attention; it will be, in a sense, the mirror of our own" (ibid.: 122). Saleem does become, in a sense, the text upon which India's history is written. His face imitates the map of India (Rushdie 1981: 231), and his body cracks in sympathy with the partition of Pakistan and other states from the once unified body of India. Moreover, he places himself at the center, as either cause or effect, of great upheavals in the history of the new country: the war between India and Pakistan (Rushdie 1981: 338); the death of Nehru (ibid.: 279); the violence that resulted in the partition of the state of Bombay (ibid.: 192).

If Saleem and India are "handcuffed" (Rushdie 1981: 9) together, then the form of Saleem's narrative is what provides a structure for both personal and private history:

As a people, we are obsessed with correspondences. Similarities between this and that, between apparently unconnected things, make us clap our hands delightedly when we find them out. It is a sort of national longing for form – or perhaps simply an expression of our deep belief that forms lie hidden within reality; that meaning reveals itself only in flashes. Hence our vulnerability to omens. . . .

(Rushdie 1981: 300)

47

Saleem does, in fact, want to explore all the correspondences, and through these to find that history is whole:

> And there are so many stories to tell, too many, such an excess of intertwined lives events miracles places rumours, so dense a commingling of the improbable and the mundane! I have been a swallower of lives; and to know me, just the one of me, you'll have to swallow the lot as well.

(Rushdie 1981: 9)

What he discovers, however, is that history will not conform to the traditional linear model into which he tries to force it. Nor will he ever be able to see it whole, or to make it whole for his readers. Instead, history is discontinuous, aleatory, fragmented.

Saleem's grandfather, Dr Aadam Aziz, first saw his future bride as a patient through a circular hole cut in a bedsheet. As different parts of his patient needed attention, the hole was strategically placed over the afflicted area, hiding the rest. This becomes a guiding metaphor for Saleem and, eventually, a way of imposing a structure, however fragmented and incomplete, on his experience. Thus, when his memory of the chronology of certain events fails, it is because his perception, and the exigencies of memory, point to multiple ways of seeing. Saleem points out that memory has its own truth: "It selects, eliminates, alters, exaggerates, minimizes, glorifies, and vilifies also; but in the end it creates its own reality" (Rushdie 1981: 211). For example, having reported the death of Gandhi, Saleem discovers that "The assassination of Mahatma Gandhi occurs, in these pages, on the wrong date. But I cannot say, now, what the actual sequence of events might have been; in my India, Gandhi will continue to die at the wrong time" (Rushdie 1981: 166). He goes on to ask a very "Ricksian" question: "Does one error invalidate the entire fabric?" (ibid.: 166). The answer, of course, must be no, since the way in which history is remembered or known will vary from account to account. Gandhi did die at a precise moment. The event, however, generates other *histories* so that for Saleem, as for others, the occasion is inextricably bound up forever with a moment of his own private history.

In many ways, *Midnight's Children* fulfils Realist dictates. It is remarkably detailed, includes "lower-class" characters, has "real" referents, specific dates, and an individual "hero" who, if not heroic in the traditional sense, certainly sees himself as an influence on and even cause of important events around him. However, one of the issues raised by the novel is the inability of Realism to communicate reality, particularly in its insistence on a unified individual subject as prime mover of events. Saleem associates himself with India, and tries to see them both as fixed entities, with himself as a major instigator of the development of the nation's history. Yet, the central position Saleem wishes to occupy in history is constantly undermined, particularly because his very identity, the single, fixed identity which is apparently causing history to take a certain course, is, like India, fluid and various. There is no more a single Saleem than there is a single India.

The most obvious manifestation of both Saleem's affinity with India and his decentered identity is in his physical cracking and splitting: he loses part of a finger, part of his scalp, and his body develops hairline cracks. This mirrors the partition of India into different states as well as the "huge gaping fissures" (Rushdie 1981: 39) that appear in the land when the rains fail. He is also, however, denied the constants by which identity is measured. Naming, for example, is a way of unifying and fixing identity. When Saleem's grandmother, Reverend Mother, begins to punctuate her sentences with the term "whatsitsname" (Rushdie 1981: 41), he writes: "I like to think of it as an unconscious cry for help . . . as a seriously-meant question. Reverend Mother was giving us a hint that, for all her presence and bulk, she was adrift in the universe. She didn't know, you see, what it was called" (ibid.: 41). By the same token, the naming of several of the characters in the novel points out that identity itself is "adrift." Re-naming is re-inventing (ibid.: 66), and characters are constantly being re-named by themselves or others: Nadir Khan becomes Lal Quasim, Naseem Aziz becomes Reverend Mother, Mumtaz Aziz becomes Amina Sinai. Saleem himself is alternately "Snotnose, Stainface, Sniffer, Baldy, Piece-of-the-Moon" (Rushdie 1981: 118). He believes that "Our names contain our fates" (ibid.: 304), but when he tries to fix his identity and his fate through the etymology of his name, he is faced with multiplicity:

Sinai contains Ibn Sina, master magician, Sufi adept; and also Sin the moon. . . . But Sin is also the letter S, as sinuous as a snake. . . . Sinai, when in Roman script, though not in Nastaliq, is also the name of the place-of-revelation . . . it is the name of the desert – of barrenness.

(Rushdie 1981: 304–5)

A further undercutting of his centrality is that the parents whose name he bears are not his parents. Born, in fact, to Vanita and Wee Willie Winkie, not to Ahmed and Amina Sinai, his real father is an Englishman, William Methwold. Saleem's future ayah, in a private revolutionary act, takes the son of the poor Vanita and Willie and switches him with that of the wealthy Ahmed and Amina Sinai. His name, then, is not his name, and his parents are not his parents.

Another comment on Realist techniques is made through the novel's proliferation of film vocabulary and metaphors. Saleem attempts to make verbal images visual ones because, as he says, "I'm bound to say that if you think of me purely as a radio, you'll only be grasping half the truth. Thought is as often pictorial or purely emblematic as verbal" (Rushdie 1981: 219). In order, then, to make his narrative visual he uses verbal versions of representational techniques of film such as "close-up" (ibid.: 32), "long-shot" (ibid.: 33), "zooming out" (ibid.: 237), and "fade out" (ibid.: 237) among others. As he points out, "nobody from Bombay should be without a basic film vocabulary" (ibid.: 33). As he tries to communicate the whole of history, so does he try to do so by making it sensual and material. Film, then, becomes one way of imposing a metaphoric structure and a vocabulary on his story. However, it is again an attempt to communicate the whole of "reality" which, of course, he cannot do. Despite his cinematic techniques, the novel is written, not filmed, and the attempts at sense-ationalism are made in words, not pictures. To some extent, though, Saleem is the camera through whose eye we "see" the story. Reading, after all, is a visual activity. But the eye, like the camera, is selective. In the same way as Aadam Aziz saw only parts of his future bride, so can Saleem see only a fragment of India's histories. The camera eye's process of selection and of framing implies a narrative comment rather than an objective view.

Despite his effort to make his story approximate "real life," Saleem is none the less conscious of narrating and of being a narrative construct. Intertextual references to *Tristram Shandy,*

A Thousand and One Nights, The Tin Drum, and *A Passage to India* make it clear that his story is drawn from other texts, both historical and literary. He also describes himself, as a developing fetus, in narrative terms: "What had been (at the beginning) no bigger than a full stop had expanded into a comma, a sentence, a paragraph, a chapter; now it was bursting into more complex developments, becoming, one might say, a book – perhaps an encyclopaedia – even a whole language" (Rushdie 1981: 100). That typical metafictive textual imagery of black/white oppositions reinforces this *written* status of *Midnight's Children*. Ahmed Sinai's change of pigmentation gives Saleem "a snow-white father to set beside my ebony mother" (Rushdie 1981: 178), just as his biological parents are black (Vanita) and white (Methwold). In this sense, then, he is the very child of print, of those black letters on white pages.

The strong and overt fantasy element in *Midnight's Children* is one indication that objectivity of narration is impossible. Saleem makes sense of an incomprehensible and horrific "reality" by giving it a metaphoric form. He creates a mythology to explain what cannot be understood rationally. This appears to be contrasted with the way his uncle, Hanif Aziz, deals with "reality" in his film scripts. Hanif dedicates himself "against everything that smacks of the unreal" (Rushdie 1981: 243). He decides that his task must be to write about "ordinary people and social problems" (ibid.: 242), and to this end he writes a script about the "Ordinary Life of a Pickle Factory" (ibid.: 242). It is about a pickle factory run entirely by women, and sections of the script describe the formation of a trade union and the minutiae of creating the perfect recipe for chutney (Rushdie 1981: 244). None of his scripts is produced, however, because, as his wife puts it, they are "boring-boring" (ibid.: 242). She begs him to add dances, exotic locations, and drama, and his studio suggests including a love scene, but Hanif, seeing these as part of the "temple of illusions" (Rushdie 1981: 244) that is the Bombay film industry, refuses. Hanif's aim is to dispel illusion, although his "reality" is as clearly a construct as that of the Bombay melodramas he so despises. He chooses to exclude dances, love scenes, and drama, and in doing so creates a *fragment* of "reality," when he thinks he is presenting a complete view. Saleem, too, creates a pickle factory run entirely by women, and while he describes the factory and its environs (Rushdie 1981:

209), as well as the raw materials needed for chutney: "fruit, vegetables, fish . . . memories, dreams, ideas" (ibid.: 460), he too is making a selection. Like the camera eye, they are both "Condemned . . . to a life of fragments" (ibid.: 121).

Midnight's Children raises two closely related issues which are central to historiographic metafiction: subjectivity and the ontology of "real" characters who appear in fictional works. In the nineteenth-century historical novel, "real" people, places, and events were included or alluded to in order to convince the reader of the "truth" of the fictional ones. In historiographic metafiction, however, the focus has shifted radically. Instead of historical characters and events proving the truth of the fiction, they point to the indeterminacy of historical knowledge.[1] Yet that *events* are indeterminate (in the sense of not being always verifiable) is not as problematic as the suggestion that historical *personages* might be treated in the same way. In *Midnight's Children*, specific references are made to Indira Gandhi, the (then) Prime Minister of India. Some of these are historically verifiable, such as: "Mrs. Indira Gandhi was born in November 1917 to Kamala and Jawaharlal Nehru. Her middle name was Priyadarshini. She was not related to 'Mahatma' M.K. Gandhi; her surname was the legacy of her marriage, in 1952, to one Feroze Gandhi, who became known as 'the nation's son-in-law'" (Rushdie 1981: 421). Other references, however, are clearly in the province of fiction. For example: "*Indira is India and India is Indira* . . . but might she not have read her own father's letter to a midnight child, in which her own, sloganized centrality was denied; in which the role of mirror-of-the-nation was bestowed on me?" (ibid.: 427). Both statements are made, however, in the context of a novel, and each is narrated by a fictional character. Is one, then, more or less "true" than the other?

The issue is an important one, and is highlighted by the libel suit, against the defamation of her son, Sanjay, that Mrs Gandhi brought against Salman Rushdie and his publishers, Jonathan Cape and Pan. Mrs Gandhi was said by her counsel to have been "horrified" by a "cruel attack" (*The Guardian*, August 1, 1984: 2) made in the following passage: "It has often been said that Mrs. Gandhi's younger son Sanjay accused his mother of being responsible, through her neglect, for his father's death [from a heart seizure] and that this gave him an unbreakable hold over her so that she became incapable of denying him anything" (Rushdie 1981: 421). In 1984, a London high court ruled in favor of Mrs Gandhi. Rushdie was ordered to read out a public apology in open court, and his publishers agreed to remove the offending passage "from all future editions over which they had control" (*Guardian*, August 1, 1981: 2).

The court's ruling certainly echoes the humanist assumption (which the novel itself contradicts) that identity is constituted extra-linguistically. It assumes, therefore, that the "Indira Gandhi" who appears in the novel *is* Indira Gandhi, and that the novel is thus a transcription of an historical reality unmediated by language. In this sense, it is a Realist judgement because it assumes a direct mimetic relationship between art and life. Fictional reference, however, is rather more complex than the court ruling would seem to suggest. As Patricia Waugh argues in *Metafiction*, fiction is "quasi-referential" in that it "can never imitate or 'represent' the world, but always imitates or 'represents' the discourses which in turn construct that world. However, because the medium of all literary fiction is language, the 'alternative worlds' of fiction, as of any other universe of discourse, can never be totally autonomous" (1984: 100). In light of this, we cannot say that "Indira Gandhi" is categorically *not* Indira Gandhi. After all, despite the arbitrariness of the linguistic sign, whose meaning is determined by social consensus rather than by innate identity, we have none the less agreed that the configuration of letters I-N-D-I-R-A G-A-N-D-H-I refers to the former Prime Minister of India. Or, more specifically, to the discourse within/by which she is defined as such and contextualized, since we cannot know Mrs Gandhi (especially today) except through the discourses of the media or history texts. In *Midnight's Children*, a novel which foregrounds the indeterminacy of both history and identity, and which self-consciously flaunts its textuality, "Indira Gandhi" is a construct with the same ontological status as Saleem Sinai. There was *an* Indira Gandhi, born in November 1917 to Kamala and Jawaharlal Nehru. There is also an "Indira Gandhi" to whom "Sanjay" made the statement that precipitated the lawsuit. Any historical event or person, then, is recontextualized by the very act of writing, whether it is the writing of history or of fiction.

For the Realists, neither reference nor subjectivity were

complicated issues. The Realists, as well as many of their critical and literary descendants, equated the presentation of the "real" with the revelation of the "true." The transcription of the "real" was *technically* unproblematic because language was perceived as transparent, and *ideologically* neutral because of a belief in a shared notion of what constituted both "reality" and "truth." In that Realism was (and is) a humanist aesthetic, meaning was perceived as emanating from Man *prior* to language. Man's function (like Adam's) was to label, or give a name to, pre-existing essences. In practice, we can see this in the Realists' privileging of biographical criticism as a means to a clearer understanding of art. Critics such as F. R. Leavis also placed great emphasis on the reader, but only on the reader who could apprehend the author's already-formulated meaning. This reader would be one of what some would see as a privileged elite, who would share with the author a common sense of values, life, art, and genius. In *Critical Practice*, Catherine Belsey summarizes these shared tenets of "common sense:"

> Common sense proposes a *humanism* based on an *empiricist-idealist* interpretation of the world. In other words, common sense urges that 'man' is the origin and source of meaning, of action, and of history (*humanism*). Our concepts and our knowledge are held to be the product of experience (*empiricism*), and this experience is preceded and interpreted by the mind, reason or thought, the property of a transcendent human nature whose essence is the attribute of each individual (*idealism*). These propositions, radically called in question by the implications of post-Saussurean linguistics, constitute the basis of a practice of reading which assumes, whether explicitly or implicitly, the theory of expressive realism. This is the theory that literature reflects the *reality* of experience as it is perceived by one (especially gifted) individual, who *expresses* it in a discourse which enables other individuals to recognize it as true.
>
> (Belsey 1980: 7)

One of the most serious challenges to the humanist conception of the individual as the autonomous source of meaning has been in the structural and post-structural positing of the individual as "subject." As we have seen in *Midnight's Children*, the issues of individuality and identity are vital for historiographic metafiction, which simultaneously creates and subverts the Realist convention of an unproblematically constituted, individual "subject" who is the prime mover of events, and from whom essential meaning emanates. The remainder of this chapter will focus on three historiographic metafictions, Peter Ackroyd's *Hawksmoor*, Nigel Williams' *Star Turn*, and Ian Watson's *Chekhov's Journey*, each of which challenges Realist concepts of "subjectivity" as defined by humanism. The notion of "subjectivity" is both difficult and complicated, and in order to fully explore it in the novels a theoretical digression will follow here, not only as an attempt to understand "subjectivity," but also as an attempt to clarify the usefulness of the concept for the study of literature.

"Subjectivity," in the sense that it is used by structural and post-structural theorists such as Catherine Belsey, Emile Benveniste, or Louis Althusser, does not have the connotation, as it tends to in traditional literary studies, of personal and private interpretation imposed on a text. Nor does it refer to an individual's self-knowledge in the sense of positing a transparent, non-contradictory self or "I." This last formulation has what Kaja Silverman in *The Subject of Semiotics* calls its most "classic demonstration" (1983: 127) in René Descartes' *Discourse on Method*:

> I became aware that, while I decided thus to think that everything was false, it followed necessarily that I who thought thus, must be something; and observing that this truth *I think, therefore I am*, was so certain and so evident, that all the most extravagant suppositions of the sceptics were not capable of shaking it. I judged that I could accept it without scruple as the first principle of the philosophy I was seeking.
>
> (Descartes 1968: 53–4)

In this (idealist) first principle, Descartes sees the "I" of his discourse as being formed by self-observation and self-examination independent of historical or linguistic circumstances. Language, here, reflects a transcendental reality; it does not mediate or create that reality. In the works of the theorists mentioned above, subjectivity is not a fixed, pre-linguistic essence, but an open *process* which, as Catherine Belsey explains, is "perpetually in the process of construction, thrown into crisis by alteration in language and in the social formation" (1980: 65).

In *Problems in General Linguistics*, Emile Benveniste discusses the specifically linguistic basis of subjectivity, drawing particularly on the structuralist formulations that language is a system of differences and that the linguistic sign is arbitrary. In the chapter "Subjectivity in Language," he argues that language is the very basis of subjectivity because only in language can the speaker designate himself or herself as "I." "I" is not, however, a term which has a single referent in language. Any speaker can be an "I" and that "I" is also constantly shifting in the sense that it can only exist in relationship to "not I:" "I use *I* only when I am speaking to someone who will be a *you* in my address. It is this condition of dialogue that is constitutive of *person*, for it implies that reciprocally *I* becomes *you* in the address of the one who in his turn designates himself as *I*" (Benveniste 1971: 224–5). In this sense, these personal pronouns are more problematic than any other linguistic articulation. The sign "I," for example, cannot refer to every individual in the same discourse, nor even to a static concept of "individual:"

> Then, what does *I* refer to? To something very peculiar which is exclusively linguistic: *I* refers to the act of individual discourse in which it is pronounced, and by this it designates the speaker. It is a term that cannot be identified except in what we have called elsewhere an instance of discourse and that has only a momentary reference. The reality to which it refers is the reality of the discourse. It is in the instance of discourse in which *I* designates the speaker that the speaker proclaims himself as the "subject." And so it is literally true that the basis of subjectivity is in the exercise of language. If one really thinks about it, one will see that there is no other objective testimony to the identity of the subject except that which he himself thus gives about himself.
>
> (Benveniste 1971: 226)

This clearly questions the humanist assumption of individual human essence, expressed in (and thus prior to) language.

In discussing Lacanian psychoanalysis, Catherine Belsey explains that a child will identify with the first-person pronoun in order to distinguish itself from others, and in order to communicate its wants and desires. Subsequently, "it learns to recognize itself in a series of subject-positions ('he' or 'she', 'boy' or 'girl', and so on) which are the positions from which discourse is intelligible to itself and others. . . . Subjectivity, then, is linguistically and discursively constructed and displaced across the range of discourses in which the concrete individual participates" (Belsey 1980: 60–1). The humanist interpretation of literature encourages the reader to "identify" with the subject-position of the narrative "I." The purpose of this is usually didactic; reader and character are put in the same ontological space so that the reader may learn from the character's moral successes and failures. The reader becomes the subject *of* this didacticism, and at the same time is subjected *to* the ideology of the text. As we have seen in *Midnight's Children*, this position is complicated when the narrative "I" is constantly shifting and changing.

One of the most serious criticisms lodged against humanism is that it presents itself as ideologically neutral. Reading and interpretation are seen as natural responses to the text. Language, because transparent, is not in itself a determining part of this response except as a medium or vehicle for meaning. However, as we have seen, language can never be neutral. Rather, "it is possible to argue that in so far as language is a way of articulating experience, it necessarily participates in *ideology*, the sum of the ways in which people both live and represent to themselves their relationship to the conditions of their existence. Ideology is *inscribed in signifying practices* – in discourses, myths, presentations and re-presentations of the way 'things' 'are' – and to this extent it is inscribed in the language" (Belsey 1980: 42). Ideology in this sense, then, is not an "optional extra" (ibid.: 5). It is inscribed in the presuppositions which inform everything we do.

Each "social formation,"[2] including literary studies, has its own discourses, and therefore its own vocabulary – what is often deprecatingly called "jargon" by those outside or unfamiliar with it. In that the individual is inscribed in language (in the same way as are the ideas which inform a social formation), the individual becomes the subject of, as well as subjected to, those ideas in the very language that creates them. This is a position ignored by both humanists and Benveniste. Those same subject-positions mentioned earlier (boy, girl, he, she, etc.) will in part determine the place of the subject within a signifying practice or social formation. When the subject posits himself or herself as "I" he or she is within an ideology of which he or she may not be aware. Indeed, ideology is powerful precisely because of its invisibility.

For example, a member of a capitalist economy must be persuaded (in order for the system to function) that he or she has a free choice of commodities on the market. Even more important, he or she must be convinced that his/her desire is under his/her control rather than created by the market. An individual who says "I have free choice" is therefore part of the discourse of a capitalist economy. As "I," he or she is the subject of the discourse to which he or she specifically refers, but also is subjected to a hidden ideology which appears simply to be the neutral and natural way "things are." The illusion of freedom is further propagated because the market *seems* to recognize the subject's autonomy. This shifts his/her attention away from the subject's participation in the maintenance of "the authority of the social formation represented in ideology as the Absolute Subject (God, the king, the boss, Man, conscience)" (Belsey 1980: 62). The consumer as subject does not see himself/herself as *subjected* to the power of the dominant ideology but instead perceives himself/herself as the very locus of free choice.

Power structures are clearly important in the "subjectification" of the individual. In "Ideology and Ideological State Apparatuses," Louis Althusser defines Ideological State Apparatuses (ISAs) as those social forces (church, school, family, culture, etc.) which work covertly to ensure this submission of the subject to the ruling ideology (1971: 132–33). Althusser cites education (school) in particular as a "subjectifying" institution. It is dominant precisely because "it is so silent" (Althusser 1971: 155) in that it pretends a position devoid of ideology. It teaches a kind of humanism which is sanctioned by the dominant (bourgeois) powers: "where teachers respectful of the 'conscience' and 'freedom' of the children who are entrusted to them (in complete confidence) by their 'parents' (who are free too, i.e. the owners of their children) open up for them the path to the freedom, morality and responsibility of adults by their own example, by knowledge, literature and their 'liberating' virtues" (Althusser 1971: 156–7). This is also clearly the path to "subjectification."

Ideology "interpellates" individuals as subjects (ibid.: 173), but this is not a function of individual choice. In fact, Althusser stresses that we are "always already subjects" (ibid.: 172). Because ISAs efface their own ideological status, and purport instead to reflect the world "as it is" in their processes, there are, then, unquestioned assumptions which effectively label the subject even before birth. Even the most basic label – whether a child is male or female, for example – will in part determine the way it is treated by the state, since there are apparently obvious and different ways to treat males and females. By presenting their practices as obvious, then, ISAs contribute to the reproduction of the relations of power.

Althusser's argument could, perhaps, be interpreted as a case for determinism. After all, if ideology is invisible, yet is inscribed in the language which also creates subjectivity, then how can we communicate anything outside ideology? How can new ideas come about in a predetermined language? Such a criticism could only be made, however, from a position which believed that words can only have a single meaning, and this is clearly not the case. Subjectivity, like meaning, is plural, and in the tensions and differences between subjectivities, social change can take place. The "I" which refers to its own position in discourse, moreover, also implies the possibility of self-reflexivity about that discourse. Feminism, for example, has challenged the related ways society refers to women, pointing out that there are ideological assumptions behind using "he" as the universal, "neutral" gender, or behind distinguishing married from unmarried women in our forms of address, Mrs and Miss. Structuralism and post-structuralism have similarly questioned our most basic assumptions about what is "natural," and "normal," and has a "common sense" to all.

In demystifying the creative and critical processes, these theories have made it possible to look at literature *and* criticism as constructed in ideology. Literature, because constructed in language, is not a privileged form of discourse, and therefore has no special claims as an emissary of "truth." Looking at literature in terms of ideology, discourse, and subjectivity also involves examining the artificial boundaries created by the academic institution between various disciplines. Having to draw on philosophy, sociology, history, and psychology (because postmodern fiction demands it) forces us to consider what constitutes "literature" as well as our ideological preconceptions of it. Postmodern novels, then, are part of the reason that all these issues need serious attention.

Star Turn, Hawksmoor, and *Chekhov's Journey* are all novels which deal specifically with ideas of subjectivity, and particularly with the subject in history. Yet they are also novels which comment on the ideological preconceptions which create categories. All three play with Realist conventions, but, more importantly, with convention in general. For example, *Hawksmoor* uses the conventions of the detective story, yet it is clearly not the popular form we usually associate with Agatha Christie or Dorothy L. Sayers. The mystery is never revealed; in fact, it is complicated by the ending. The novel is also vehemently anti-empirical, which is to say it is against the classic detective's primary means for solving a murder. *Chekhov's Journey* is a novel about a proposed television rendition of an incident in Chekhov's life. Yet the researchers' attempts to re-create the past rely on hypnotism of the actor portraying Chekhov, rather than on documents. While trying to find the past, they are caught up in a space-science-fiction-fantasy future. Of these three novels, Nigel Williams' *Star Turn* is the one which most overtly thematizes the political and ideological theories of "subjectification."

Superficially, the novel follows the pattern of a *Bildungsroman* in the sense defined by M. H. Abrams: "The subject of these novels is the development of the protagonist's mind and character, as he passes from childhood through varied experiences – and usually through a spiritual crisis – into maturity and the recognition of his identity and role in the world" (1971: 112–13). This implies the development of control over and knowledge of one's identity, and a clear recognition of the forces which formed it. One's personal history, here, is seen in unproblematic relationship to the static self one attains and maintains. The pattern of cause and effect is clearly delineated: the past is a knowable entity unmediated by the caprices of memory or the layering of experience.

The story of Amos Barking and Isaac Rabinowitz appears to follow this pattern. Amos, the narrator, tells the story of his and his friend's extravagant adventures with historical figures such as

Lenin, Marcel Proust, Sigmund Freud, and General Haig among others. Amos writes the novel while working for the British government as a propagandist during the Second World War. His cynicism and cavalier attitude toward the importance of his job anger his head of department who arranges for Amos to witness the bombing of Dresden. This lesson is designed to show Amos the "reality" of war and, by extension, the unmediated "reality" of *all* experience. It is intended to add sincerity to his character and to his novel and propaganda writing. However, the novel is also the story of Isaac, and it is through his story that we see why this attempt to create an epiphany which will reveal Amos' true identity to himself is highly problematic.

Star Turn begins with a parody of the confident Cartesian "I:" "I am what I remember. Nothing else. Always assuming, of course, that I can remember what it is I am" (Williams 1985: 11). It is memory, here, which creates the individual and, as we have seen in previously discussed novels, both personal and collective memories are suspect in their ability to re-create the whole past. Amos' memory re-invents the past to an extent which even he finds alarming: "Yesterday, for example, I became convinced, at about ten in the morning, that I had had my appendix out" (Williams 1985: 11). His profession, of course, adds a further complication to his narrative, even though he tries to separate his propaganda from his art:

> I'm a skilled propagandist. I can make one German plane downed over the Channel sound like the end of the line for the Reich, but because of this artistic scruple of mine, because of this absurd and impractical desire to remember correctly, I am determined not to write propaganda for myself. I am going to rise above what I have become, transform myself into a truth teller.
>
> (Williams 1985: 17)

The wilful distortion of events in his job is something Amos finds increasingly difficult: only through memory can he come to the "truth," although this is always conditioned by his faulty memory and penchant for lying. However, what Amos as fiction writer points out is that nothing is impervious to ideological manipulation and subjectification, particularly in politics and war.

Initially, we are told, the novel is to be Isaac's story, and for this reason, the narrator tries to efface himself taking Tessa's suggestion that: "When you write about it . . . you must write about *it* and forget I, I, I, I" (Williams 1985: 14). The novel's first-person narration attests to Amos' difficulty with this, although the confident "I" he tries to assert is constantly under erasure. The kind of control over identity which is common in the *Bildungsroman*, then, is posited, only to be subverted. The narrative draws attention to this primarily through Isaac who, even at the age of 8, is presented as someone with the ability to wield power: "Some of us are born to be in charge of other fellows and if we can make sure that fairness and good order prevail, in the house and on the field, there will be little to complain of as far as the School is concerned" (Williams 1985: 34). He behaves as though "his future was a subject over which he had some control" (Ibid.: 45), and his self-determination leads his father to characterize him as someone who "wants to make history. Always has. Tiny baby plays with soldiers, yes? Bigger baby walks around telling other babies what to do. A tyrant in the making, I can tell you" (Ibid.: 45). Isaac's power seems initially to bring him success and self-definition. Of the two boys, he is the leader, and he is always centered out for attention by the various historical characters with whom the two come into contact. However, Isaac's apparent centrality, gained by virtue of his self-control, is repeatedly called into question. Like Saleem Sinai in *Midnight's Children*, he is paradoxically de-centered; he is at once the subject of the novel, yet he is shown to be subjected to forces which problematize his control of his own identity.

This is signalled to the reader through the novel's concern with proper names:

> People become their names, don't you think? People called Walpurgisnacht acquire a stoop, cadaverous cheeks and hands as cold as the grave, while people called things like Weg-Prossor or Porteous-Smythe tend to have a knack for hailing taxis or bullying waiters. And such things are not merely the result of heredity. They can be learnt.
>
> (Williams 1985: 37)

Although his friend's name is *I*saac, Amos calls him Zak throughout most of the novel. By effacing the "I" in Isaac, the narrator draws attention to the problems of a concrete individual subject designated through naming. Part of Zak's power in the novel is precisely in his ability to shift his identity in order to fit into others' conceptions of him: "who precisely Zak was or where he was from was something he liked to alter to suit the needs of the moment" (Williams 1985: 37). As a child in a Christian school, he forsakes his Jewish identity, ignoring his father when he speaks Yiddish, and adopting the name Thomas Shadbolt and the appropriate manners of an English aristocrat. In adolescence he aspires to be "one of the boys," changing his manner and his accent to the point that he becomes unrecognizable as Isaac, and indistinguishable from his models.

The various roles that he adopts are part of Zak's attempt to participate in, and even create, history. He wants to act in history, no matter what the role: "You must embrace the stupidity of the times. . . . When they are hysterical you must sob and laugh with them, when the time comes to be serious – put on your solemn face. Act it out. Act it out. This history of yours is nothing but a performance" (Williams 1985: 248). Even as a self-professed "star turn" in history, however, Zak is subject to history's manipulation. His desire to perform leads him from a passion for the Communist Party to a brief rediscovery of his Jewish faith, to eventually playing Oswald Mosely's double – a role which ultimately causes his death. Far from being in control, either through the power of his personality or the skill of performance, then, Zak becomes a pawn, subjected to the manipulation of the social forces he tries to master.

By the time Zak joins the British Union of Fascists, Amos has become increasingly disenchanted with his friend's life as a social and political chameleon: "Are we hecklers? Are we for it? Are we socialists these days? Or are we tories? Or are we just after climbing on any wagon that looks good?" (Williams 1985: 263). While trying to escape ideology through his involvement with political extremes, Zak has, instead, acted out an ideological agenda which asserts the primacy of an individual action in the creation of history. It is interesting that his emphasis on action causes him to reject the textual representations of history which so involve both his father and Amos. Amos' cynicism about his friend's behavior is derived in part, then, from his experiences as journalist, propagandist, and novelist all of which rely on the textualizing, and therefore re-inventing of events. Amos' knowledge of history is mediated by representations of it from both books and films. Zak wants to be an "I-witness" to "real" history, whereas for Amos, the telling of events relies on an "eye" informed by perception, as well as by a certain self-consciousness about his penchant for telling lies. Amos too sees history, or more accurately, the *telling* of history, as a performance. Certainly the present acts on the past, and in this way, "We get the history we want" (Williams 1985: 114). His emphatic self-reflexiveness in his role as novelist, then, is a manifestation of *his* desire to be a "star turn" in history.

Despite his awareness of perception, however, Amos presents himself as simply an observer of events. He is swept along by Zak's enthusiasms, and the implication of this is that he thinks ideology only affects other people. He presents himself at once as a camera eye recording "reality," and as a propagandist re-inventing "reality" for public consumption. Interestingly, he relies on his memory of films to structure his memory of other events, and is sometimes unable to distinguish between films and his most personal recollections. At one point, for example, he remembers his mother:

> From time to time she would lift her head and listen for something, the sound of approaching planes perhaps, and then address herself to her work again. She was wearing a headscarf. It was not until I saw the headscarf that I realized that I was recalling not my mother, but a still from a film called *Make the Dinner Go Round*. God knows what my mother is doing.
>
> (Williams 1985: 189–90)

The image is more tyrannical – in that it is less open to multiplicity – than the word. It is the visual image more than the written one, after all, which influences Amos' narrative. Given this, the two methods that Alan, his boss, uses to prompt Amos into patriotic action, and out of his disrespect for the war, are especially interesting. Amos uses a pseudonym, Henry Swansea, in his job at the Ministry of Information, and, when discovered, this arouses official suspicions about his politics. A single identity, it is assumed, denotes a single loyalty. A double one indicates a spy – or at least someone who sees things, as

Henry/Amos does, from a view contrary to the dominant ideology. His antipathy to the war, therefore, raises suspicions about his role as an ideologically correct Englishman.

To test this, Alan takes him to a movie set where a propaganda film, *Swastika Dreams*, is being shot. Amos is interpolated into the film as an extra, and his reaction to the actors playing Nazis is supposed to be an indication of his attitude toward the "real" war. It will make him see what Alan calls "the lie of the land" (Williams 1985: 234). But the expression has a contradictory meaning. The film is meant to be a "true" representation, and thus promote a sincere reaction from Amos, but it is also a "lie" in the sense that it can only ever be a part of a perception within a frame created by wartime propaganda. The real test is for Amos to witness the bombing of Dresden. Like *Swastika Dreams*, this attack, as it is explained to Amos, is an exercise in propaganda, intended to demoralize the enemy and to "whip up. . . support" from the "Great British Public" (Williams 1985: 255). The sight of the burning city does make Amos realize that "*The shadows I saw were real to others. It's only tonight that I have seen history in action*" (ibid.: 289). But Amos is none the less in the contradictory position of all history writers – he has seen one moment in history, which cannot be generalized to include all historical moments:

> You can't spell away the world out there, the world of politics where ideas become reality. Looking back at what I have written I can see that that is what I have tried to do with Isaac's life, to cast it in a secret, private form, to confuse lies with truth until there seems no reality, no objective standard of truth, possible. That is, of course, a fashionable line of escape. Things happen. Whether they happened or not can be tested and discovered. To abandon that hope is to abandon hope in any kind of justice or decency. What happened last night happened. About the rest I can't say. I can plead in my defence that very often what I have written is not half so monstrously absurd as what occurred over Dresden.
>
> (Williams 1985: 307)

Alan wants Amos to take a stand (a particular stand) on the war, and to come to terms with his identity – in short, to mature through spiritual crisis. Yet Amos' dilemma is one which is shared by the reader: the "real" experiences of both *Swastika Dreams* and of Dresden can only be known textually by the reader. Left in his office to explain away Dresden and to come to terms with his reaction to it, Amos finds himself in a quandary. He tries to create an active role for himself, to accept the "actuality of an individual, a nation" (Williams 1985: 311). But the ideology which created Zak, the primacy of individual action, is not one he can accept, particularly since the action over Dresden caused so much suffering. All he can do is textualize himself (as he has done with the "shadows" of previous events) as a writer of absurd propaganda: "We went in over that Nazi stronghold, the city of *Dresden*, and really gave it what for. Nazi cats and dogs suffered too as – " (Williams 1985: 313). Unable to make a commitment either to action or concrete identity, his final line is a plea to the reader: "Make it all go away, somebody, can't you?" (ibid.: 314). It is the reader, then, who has to make the final decision about Amos' identity in taking action to close the book.

The problems of ideology and subjectivity are highlighted in *Star Turn* because of the omnipresence of war. Against the background of crude polarities (us/them, good/evil, German destruction/British liberalism), identity is supposed to be easily determined through ideological commitment. However, this would assume precisely the kind of "objective standard of truth" which Amos finds so difficult to concede, and which, the novel points out, is so problematic. Although it uses the *Bildungsroman* structure superficially, *Star Turn* undermines the humanist ideology behind the genre. The characters are subjected to the manifestations of history and politics rather than being in control of them. History, here, does not build to a crescendo which leads to spiritual awareness, but is instead fragmented and ruptured. Similarly, Peter Ackroyd's *Hawksmoor* is concerned with the way in which genre defines subjectivity.

Soon after the discovery of the theft in Wilkie Collins' *The Moonstone*, the investigating sergeant teaches his associate one of the rules of the game. In referring to a previous case he notes: "At one end of the inquiry there was a murder, and at the other end there was a spot of ink on the tablecloth that nobody could account for. In all my experience along the dirtiest ways of this dirty little world, I have never met with such a thing as a trifle yet" (Collins 1966: 136). In the classic English detective novel, the impetus for detection lies in the mystery behind the "trifle." Who indeed can account for this signifier wrenched from its signified? What is seen as the usual transparency of human communication, in these stories, is criminally ruptured, resulting in a chaos of "semantic ambiguity" (Moretti 1983: 147). The detective's job is to heal the rupture by tracing back through history for its origins which, when discovered, will aid in re-establishing the harmonious conditions of causality and legality which existed prior to the crime. The crime, then, is not just a crime against an individual, but against a whole social order of communication and signification. Through reason and empirical research, of course, the univocal truth will be told and order restored; if Sherlock Holmes looks at the ink spot long enough, after all, he will eventually reconstruct the whole novel.

Rupture, in detective fiction, is clearly a social evil. Because it is an innately conservative genre, it deplores absence and, as Todorov points out in *The Poetics of Prose*, the history of the crime is an absent text (1977: 44–6). The story of detection is the story of the book itself – it is a promise of closure, linearity, and a return to common sense. All of this is achieved through a process of subject formation; through filling in the gap with the name of the offender. This naming interpellates the criminal back into the ideology he or she has sought to transgress. The detective, then, becomes a guardian of ideology, and his or her considerable power lies in being able to turn the traces of the crime into monuments to individuality and teleological history.

The detective story's highly stylized and strictly monitored conventions attest to the conservatism of the genre. The Detection Club of London enforced this through a sort of Hippocratic oath sworn by its mystery writer members. The purpose of this was to ensure that the detective novel "play fair with" its reader, and thus members of the club agreed to "seemly moderation" in the use of "Gangs, Conspiracies, Death Rays, Ghosts, Hypnotism and Chinamen" (Holquist 1971: 142), and to "utterly and forever forswear Mysterious Poisons Unknown to Science" (Haycraft 1941: 198), "Divine Revelation, Feminine Intuition, Mumbo Jumbo, Jiggery Pokery or the Act of God" (Symons 1985: 13). Since the reader of detective fiction generally is well aware of the conventions, he or she is also implicated as a co-producer of the return to order, and as a member of the club which is able to write sexism and racism into its very constitution. In this way it reproduces the conditions of its production. What happens then, in the anti-detective novel – what William Spanos has called "the paradigmatic archetype of postmodern literary imagination" (1972: 54) – when it appropriates a genre which is a model not only of ideological hegemony, but of literary conservatism?

The presence/absence duality that Todorov sees at the heart of the classic detective novel is one which is equally essential in a postmodern historiographic metafiction such as Peter Ackroyd's *Hawksmoor*. The novel has a double plot composed of a series of parallel eighteenth- and twentieth-century murders. Those in the eighteenth century are committed by Sir Christopher Wren's colleague, Nicholas Dyer. Dyer is an architect responsible for building seven new churches in London and, as part of a Satanic and Faustian pact, he consecrates his churches with sacrificial victims. The twentieth-century murders are almost identical to the ones committed by Dyer. Most of the victims have the same names as their eighteenth-century counterparts, they die at the same churches and in the same sequence. Yet these are, ultimately, crimes without a subject; no traces are left of the murderer, and not even the time of death can be verified in any individual case. Like his classic counterparts, the novel's modern detective, Nicholas Hawksmoor, tries to solve the crimes by ratiocination. Assuming the murders to be committed by an individual, he looks for what the received knowledge of his experience tells him: "no human being could rest or move in any area without leaving some trace of his or her identity" (Ackroyd 1985: 114). He spends his time searching for patterns and structures, but what patterns he finds, which seem to be traces of identification, and recurrence, lead nowhere, and eventually Hawksmoor begins to lose his reason – to hear strange voices and to see visions. Finally, he realizes that the structure he has been looking for has an archi-*textual* symmetry which is completed by his own death at the end of the novel.

The absence at the heart of this text is of precisely the kind of identity secured through naming, and through which the illusion of individual, essential meaning is created. The question "*who* dunnit?" cannot be answered here because there is no solution, and it is solution that presupposes a subject. *Hawksmoor* sets up the conventions of a classic detective novel whose certainties it then subverts, and in doing so, it questions the apparently unproblematic way in which the detective comes to reconstruct history and *his* story through trifles. One of the commonplaces of detective fiction is its backward construction. The author has to formulate the solution before he or she can strategically place the clues. The reader's assumption, then, has to be that the amassing of evidence is actually leading somewhere, and that the past and the present are in unproblematic correspondence. In *Hawksmoor*, the compilation of apparent clues is overwhelming. Even apart from the murders, hardly a gesture or conversation occurs without being repeated. Yet this doubling, which in a detective novel would lead to accumulation and closure, leads in *Hawksmoor* to ambiguity and difference. This is most obvious with respect to Dyer and Hawksmoor themselves. They live in the same area of London, Dyer has his offices in Scotland Yard as does Hawksmoor, Dyer's assistant is Walter Pyne, Hawksmoor's Walter Payne, and when Dyer loses the notebook in which he keeps the tenets of his creed, Hawksmoor finds it. Clearly, the initial impulse is to equate the two characters, especially since, historically, the real Nicholas Hawksmoor occupied a similar position to the one Dyer occupies in the novel. It is no wonder, then, that the modern Detective Chief Inspector Hawksmoor feels both himself and his investigation to be out of time, in the wrong time, timeless. In fact, not only time but language problematizes his identity. He listens to the conversations of his colleagues, but can make no sense of them since the sequences of phrases seem to bear no relationship to one another. He repeats overheard words and phrases to himself and tries them out hesitantly on his assistant. It is a tactic, however, that is interpreted as parody, and thus is treated as senseless. Nevertheless, Hawksmoor feels subjected to and manipulated by language: "he saw no reason for the words he himself used, which came out of him like vomit, which carried him forward without rhyme or meaning" (Ackroyd 1985: 117–18). Like his historical namesake, then, he is a discursive construct, and can only be known textually, even by himself:

"The operation," he asked, "is it going according to the book?" "Yes, to the book. . . ." "But perhaps there is no book in this case . . ." . . . He was playing a part: he knew this, and believed it to be his strength. Others did not realise that their parts had been written for them, their movements already marked out like chalk lines upon a stage.

(Ackroyd 1985: 118)

Because the agenda of postmodern texts is a paradoxical one in their simultaneous presentation and subversion of Realist conventions, there is a constant tension, here, between past and present, presence and absence, construction and destruction. This is thematized in the novel as Hawksmoor himself is torn between precisely these differences. Clearly, Hawksmoor recognizes semantic ambiguity, as well as the inevitability of rupture. Yet in this case, *he* is the one constrained by a social structure, one that employs him to maintain it. Thus, when he begins to look beyond the recent, twentieth-century past, to what the reader recognizes as the eighteenth-century text, but his colleagues see as madness, he becomes a danger to the maintenance of order. After one of the murders, at the church of St Mary Woolnoth, Hawksmoor sees a tramp drawing on the pavement in chalk: "the figure of a man who had put a circular object up to his right eye and was peering through it as if it were a spyglass" (Ackroyd 1985: 162). A few pages later, the same drawing is sent to him in a letter with the message "DON'T FORGET . . . THE UNIVERSAL Architect" (ibid.: 166). Sherlock Holmes, to whom the drawing refers, is, of course, detective fiction's transcendental signifier, and it is implied here that if Hawksmoor can only understand this reference to convention – and its lesson that the past is causally and rationally constructed – then he will solve the case. However, the convention undercuts itself: the chalk drawing of Holmes is equally the outline of a dead body, a dead convention. The Universal Architect, here, can only be the reader, since it is he or she who is in possession of *all* the histories: the historically verifiable past, the eighteenth-century text and the text accumulated through reading. This is signalled by the repetition of the sign M_SE_M (museum) engraved on a building at one of the murder sites. The missing letter is "U," ("you") the reader, who is doubly implicated not only as a repository of the past, but also as a co-creator of artifact and artifice.

Hawksmoor eventually comes to see that *his* only solution has to be a creative one. The eighteenth-century text has already equated architecture and the building of a (specifically this) novel: "And so let us beginne; and, as the Fabrick takes its Shape in front of you, alwaies keep the Structure intirely in mind as you inscribe it . . . thus a book begins with a frontispiece, then its Dedication, and then its Preface or Advertisement" (Ackroyd 1985: 5). The repeated engravings that Hawksmoor sees on the churches: "Founded in the Saxon Age and Last Rebuilt by Nicholas Dyer," encourage him to a similarly textual solution – an attempt at interpretation rather than recuperation of the past:

> The event of the boy's death was not simple because it was not unique and if he traced it backwards, running the time slowly in the opposite direction . . . it became no clearer. The chain of causality might extend as far back as the boy's birth . . . or even further into the darkness beyond that. And what of the murderer, for what sequence of events had drawn him to wander by this old church? All these events were random and yet connected, part of a pattern so large that it remained inexplicable. He might, then, have to invent a past from the evidence available – and, in that case, would not the future also be an invention? It was as if he were staring at one of those puzzle drawings in which foreground and background create entirely different images: you could not look at such a thing for long.
>
> (Ackroyd 1985: 157)

The plurality here is one which underlies Hawksmoor's discovery of himself as textual construct. The foreground and background, once acknowledged as such, can never again be seen as a unified whole, but only as a constant play of differences. In this sense, naming doesn't fix Hawksmoor's identity, but only points out his difference both from Dyer, and from architect Nicholas Hawksmoor. In the novel, neither Hawksmoor nor Dyer is even given a chance to recognize himself: the mirrors that both own are convex, and thus distort the reflections, and Hawksmoor, seeing himself reflected in a shop window, cries out "Do I know you?" (Ackroyd 1985: 211). Toward the end of the novel, Hawksmoor looks Dyer up in an encyclopedia, and the citation gives him a direction toward his own end in the church of Little St Hugh, what the encyclopedia calls Dyer's finest building. Of all the churches in the novel, this is the one with no historical referent. It is pure narrative, and is described as such by Dyer as he looks at his finished plans: "the Elevation . . . is like the Symbol or Theme of a Narrative . . . the Upright of the Front . . . is like to the main part of a Story . . . the many and irregular Doors, Stairways and Passages like so many Ambiguous Expressions, Tropes, Dialogues and Metaphoricall speeches" (Ackroyd 1985: 205). It is in this church, appropriately enough, that Dyer and Hawksmoor meet their ends: Dyer, because he has fulfilled the conditions of his Satanic pact, Hawksmoor, because he has fulfilled the obligations of his literary one. The lyricism of the ending, in a sort of Druid dance, fosters a deliberate evasiveness and contradiction:

> and I must have slept, for all these figures greeted me as if they were in a dream. The light behind them effaced their features and I could see only the way they turned their heads, both to left and to right. The dust covered their feet and I could see only the direction of their dance, both backwards and forwards. And when I went among them, they touched fingers and formed a circle around me; and, as we came closer, all the while we moved further apart. Their words were my own but not my own, and I found myself on a winding path of smooth stones. And when I looked back, they were watching one another silently.

> (Ackroyd 1985: 217)

It could be a reference to the supernatural – the novel, in fact, plays with this as a possibility, especially since the pattern formed by drawing a line between all these churches is a pentangle (ibid.: 186). The reference itself is contradictory, though, because a foray into the spirit world would imply a human essence, and *Hawksmoor* disputes this as either a spiritual or a literary possibility. Out of the dance comes a repetition of several of the novel's images, especially those of doubling, identity, and dreams, but there is no pattern here *except* for the very play of frolicking signifiers. Instead, the mystery is maintained, if not complicated, by the novel's self reference, naming itself as the ultimate culprit.

In *Signs Taken for Wonders*, Franco Moretti calls detective fiction a hymn to coercive culture: "This culture knows, orders and defines all the significant data of individual existence as part of social existence. Every story reiterates Bentham's Panopticon ideal: the model prison that signifies the metamorphosis of liberalism into total scrutability" (1983: 143). The classic detective novel does indeed enforce a kind of discipline, one which prefers and enacts the literary and social order ideology demands. The discipline of the detective is mind over matter, the discipline of the text is exercised in power over the reader – all the clues are apparently available, as Ellery Queen's stories remind us, even if they make no sense until the detective's authority collects them into meaningful patterns.

In postmodern texts, the very structure echoes what Hawksmoor refers to as the foreground/background puzzle. The conventions are inscribed, the reader is expected to know them, and yet they are undercut. But is this a radical undercutting or is the postmodern text *also* a kind of prison? While the two images in the puzzle play against one another, they also inform one another. Similarly, the conventions, both literary and ideological, are re-membered by the reader; they are open to view, but not with a view to liberation from them. In this double play, therefore, the reader is in a paradoxical position: imprisoned precisely because he or she recuperates, rather than murders, ink.

As *Hawksmoor* uses conventions of the detective story, so does Ian Watson's *Chekhov's Journey* use the techniques of science fiction. This is perhaps why its questioning of the genre provoked such a dismissive review from Kelvin Johnston. In the London *Observer* he comments that the novel is "a good quick read but it's too ingenious for its own good" (Johnston 1983: 33), and that it "suffers from the common illusion. . . that to be obscure is to be mature" (ibid.: 33). These comments are interesting considering that the novel is reviewed as science fiction, and yet uses the conventions of the genre only to subvert them. Like *Hawksmoor* and *Star Turn*, *Chekhov's Journey* plays with the very notion of genre as a subjectifying process. Not only is the reader subjected to the use and abuse of familiar conventions, but the text itself becomes the subject of and subject to the normative rules of generic identity. As is the case with the previous two novels, the use of genre in this novel is contradictory if not paradoxical. On one hand, genre theory presupposes a textual identity which is fixed and unchanging – the text is named as a specific type or sub-type, and this is a determining factor in how the text is read. This is not unlike the kind of reading described as Realist in Chapter one: the reader reads the text as though charting the differences from and similarities to an ideal designation of the genre. On the other hand, historical knowledge in these texts is filtered through the genre and its particular structures. How we know history is dependent upon the form in which it is communicated. This accounts for some of the textualized confusion experienced by the characters in these texts, as we have seen in *Hawksmoor*. The detective's identity as well as his method of crime solving is problematized because, as much as he tries to behave like a classic detective, the novel undercuts this kind of empirical reasoning. He is instead bound by his nominal relationship with historical architect Nicholas Hawksmoor, as well as by his textual relationship to Nicholas Dyer.

In *Chekhov's Journey*, there is a similar confusion because of a play with time and its relation to subjectivity. In both of the other novels, time has been an issue. Both the *Bildungsroman* and the detective novel assume a world of cause and effect in which all events have a place on a linear, temporal continuum. Characters in a *Bildungsroman* are expected to learn from experience over time, and similarly, crimes in a detective story are solved through a timely accumulation of clues. In science fiction the issue is somewhat different, partly because it is a difficult genre to define. We usually associate it with a type of fiction that uses science and technology and the "marvels of discovery and achievement that may result from scientific development" (Abrams 1971: 178). J. A. Cudden defines it more soberly as a form that "deals wholly or in part with exotic, supernatural or speculative topics" (1982: 608), but recognizes that this would include texts not generally considered as science fiction such as Homer's *Odyssey* or Dante's *Divine Comedy*. For the most part, science fiction, like detective fiction, posits a norm which is under siege. Whether it is attacked by a criminal or creatures from another planet, the essential order, having been disturbed, needs to be restored. This is not always the case with science fiction, since endings may well be apocalyptic or estranging (as in *The Twilight Zone*), but there is none the less a sense of the norm which is lost. Equally, as Tzvetan Todorov argues in *The Fantastic*, the strange may be seen as being at least analogous to what is considered "normal:" "The initial data are supernatural: robots, extraterrestrial beings, the whole interplanetary context. The narrative movement consists in obliging us to see how close these apparently marvelous elements are to us, to what degree they are present in our life" (Todorov 1975: 172). Again, there is the assumption here of a shared sense of what the normal is in comparison to the marvelous.

In *Chekhov's Journey*, the sense of wonder is initially directed toward apparently extraordinary events, but becomes a metaphor for the discovery of a changing conception of how we know history. While the novel uses conventions of time travel and future worlds, it is also concerned with how we know and rewrite the past, and what effect this has on the present. The discovery of the past, in fact, is the impetus for the plot in which a Russian film crew gathers at a country retreat to write a script about Anton Chekhov's journey across Siberia to visit a convict colony in 1888.

The plot of *Chekhov's Journey* is a complex one. The film crew, trying to bring objective reality to their docu-drama of Chekhov's life, hires a psychiatrist who has developed a method of hypnosis which heightens perception. Dr Kirilenko is to hypnotize Mikhail, the actor who is to play Chekhov in the film, so that he will be able to re-create the playwright. The implication of this is that there exists a supernatural, eternal human essence to which Mikhail can "tune in," and which will add "realism" to both the script and his performance of it. Mikhail's hypnotic trances, however, belie the "single chain of cause and effect" (Watson 1983: 124) the film crew expects. He experiences, in fact, several Chekhovs, not one of whom conforms to the accepted historico-biographical notions of him. The first hypnosis reveals that Chekhov knew about the mysterious Tunguska explosion which, according to the film crew, occurred in Siberia in 1908, four years after Chekhov's death, and was the result, it is speculated, of a falling comet. Mikhail, however, reveals that Chekhov read about the incident in a newspaper in 1888, and that the site of the disaster, not the convict colony, was the aim of his journey. Subsequent hypnoses reveal yet another Chekhov, a futuristic, almost comic book character. Here, he is Commander Anton Astrov, pilot of the spaceship *K. E. Tsiolkovsky* whose mission is the colonization of a suitable star in the galaxy. When the spaceship tries to set off, though, disaster strikes and it is trapped in a time warp whose effect is to drive it backwards through time on a collision course with Siberia. The spaceship, caught between two versions of historical events, becomes *both* Tunguska explosions, crashing in 1908 *and* 1888.

Because his film is to be a way of fixing the truth, these several Chekhovs enrage Felix, the film's director, whose overwhelming desire for mimesis has led him to sponsor the "nationwide Chekhov Look-Alike contest" (Watson 1983: 14) which Mikhail won. Indeed, both Felix and Sergey, the script-writer, confuse Mikhail with Chekhov. They address the representation as though it were "reality," just as Felix wants the audience to address his film: "You adopted a modern *scientific* approach in your plays. You believed in evidence. Life was your laboratory. So you wrote scientific drama and scientific fiction. Damn it, I mean *he* did! Chekhov did" (Watson 1983: 24). Ironically, however, the rewriting of history began even before Mikhail's hypnosis. Chekhov's journey, whatever its aim, is to fit within a specific ideology, and to this end Felix and Sergey plan to show it as "brought about by an act of social commitment" (Watson 1983: 13). Not only Chekhov, but the locus of his journey has to be refashioned. Far from being merely "seas of mud and bitter frosts" (ibid.: 11), although it is precisely this in Mikhail's version of history, Siberia becomes a land of opportunity:

> Look, an underlying theme of the film has to be how Siberia spelled *space for development*. Though this didn't occur in a properly planned way till later on. . . . And as a sub-theme, there could well be a hint that the Siberia of tomorrow's world will literally be space. Outer space – the asteroid belt, the moons of Jupiter! Where a socialist attitude's the only possible one; everyone pitching in, or else it's lethal. We mustn't associate space with punishment.
>
> (Watson 1983: 12)

This mention of Siberia as "outer space" thematizes the

science-fiction aspect of the novel that is created by the distance between what the film crew perceives as "normal," and Mikhail's questioning of the norm in his performance under hypnosis. Mikhail's reading of the past, however, is as viable as the film crew's. His performance is a form of, indeed a parody of, method acting. To act Chekhov, it is implied, he must *be* Chekhov, an illusion which is fostered by the script-writer's and director's confusion of actor and role. Mikhail takes his cues from the comments made by various members of the crew, such as those about the film's concern with outer space, in order to properly play the part. His qualification for the role, besides that of his physical resemblance, is his knowledge of Chekhov's life. As the psychiatrist points out:

> "There's no point in persuading somebody that they're Leonardo or Levitan if they don't know a scrap about them. Whereas *you*", and Kirilenko fixed unerringly on Mikhail, "you know a good deal about Chekhov, eh?"
>
> The actor toyed with his moustache. "That's as maybe. . . . When you come down to brass tacks, we really haven't the foggiest about old Anton."
>
> "In which case, it'll be up to *you* to select the true interpretation. And it'll be the true one because it'll be based on your unconscious perceptions. . . ."

(Watson 1983: 25)

It is clear, here, that historical knowledge is not perceived as problematic; nor is its interpretation seen to be the result of the mediation of texts or cultural factors. Since the method of uncovering Chekhov has been chosen because of Chekhov's interest in science, the film crew imagines that its results will have a scientific accuracy, or, that through something dear to Chekhov, they will have a better chance of re-creating him. This is not unlike Geoffrey Braithwaite's pilgrimage to Flaubert's haunts hoping to get closer to his famous writer in *Flaubert's Parrot*. This naive notion of both science and history is subverted by the hypnosis itself (just as the parrot eventually subverts Braithwaite's search for truth). Mikhail's knowledge of Chekhov can only have been gained textually. It is not surprising, then, when characters similar to those in Chekhov's plays appear as "real" in Mikhail's hypnotic trances.

In "Theory of the Text" Roland Barthes argues that the notion of the "text" tends to "abolish the separation of genres and arts" (1981: 42), because texts are no longer simply messages, but "perpetual productions, enunciations through which the subject continues to struggle" (ibid.: 42). The abolition of strictly defined boundaries extends to "infinity the freedoms of reading (authorizing us to read works of the past with an entirely modern gaze, so that it is legitimate, for example, to read Sophocles' 'Oedipus' by pouring Freud's Oedipus back into it, or to read Flaubert on the basis of Proust" (Barthes 1981: 42). Since history has been discussed here as a text, Barthes' comments can also be applied to the reading of history in general, and Mikhail's reading of history in particular.

Through his trances, we can see Mikhail actually re-creating history, both past and future, imbuing it with conscious and "unconscious perceptions" from his present. If science is to be a sub-text of the film, it is appropriate (considering, too, the genre of the novel) that Mikhail should find, in one of his trances, K. E. Tsiolkovsky, the inventor of a new school of literature – "Science Fantasy" (Watson 1983: 53). Tsiolkovsky's scientific hypotheses try to explain the Tunguska explosion as one caused by a " 'ship of space' such as I envisage ought to be powered by a principle of 'jet propulsion' employing liquid fuel as the propellant" (Watson 1983: 54). Mikhail's future fantasy of Anton Astrov, pilot of the spaceship *K. E. Tsiolkovsky*, is based on his reading of the past which is in turn prompted by his perceptions of the present. In response to the film crew's confusion about these unforeseen Chekhovs, the psychiatrist explains that under hypnosis Mikhail has to fantasize "*accurately*, just as I instructed him to. He can only invent around the known facts. He doesn't have free rein to make up whatever he chooses" (Watson 1983: 46). Mikhail is, however, an actor, and from the "script" of the available information of Chekhov's life *and works* he develops a performance which is the essence of multiplicity. The "known" facts, after all, are themselves textual and thus subject to interpretations.

Mikhail's reading of history with a "modern gaze," not unexpectedly, changes the present. As the re-interpreter and performer of history, Mikhail is himself the subject of and subjected to this new interpretation. Chekhov's multiplicity, as created by Mikhail, continues even after the hypnosis is over. A volume of Chekhov's plays, discovered in the retreat's library, includes *The Apple Orchard, Uncle Ivan,* and *Three Cousins*. The *Soviet Encyclopedia* is found to list the possible events from Mikhail's hypnosis as facts. On a science-fiction level, this initially seems a kind of *Twilight Zone* nightmare, especially since the crew suspects that not only the plays but the whole social structure might well have been altered by Mikhail's re-invention of the past. However, if we read the text as a metaphor for reading history, then the change in the plays is a change in the film crew's (and the reader's) perceptions of the present brought about by a different interpretation of the past: "Past events can be altered. History gets rewritten. Well, we've just found out that this applies to the real world too. . . . Maybe the history of the world is changing constantly!" (Watson 1983: 174).

Each of the novels in this chapter deals with Realist conventions and their subversion through the representation of history. They question traditional assumptions about history and, in doing so, consider history's relation to concepts such as "truth," meaning, and subjectivity. History, however, is not the only mode where Realism is challenged. In the following chapters we will consider the mediation of Realist techniques through performance, visual art, and film; indeed, through the representation of representation itself.

Chapter three

Postmodern performance

Come, children, let us shut up the box and the puppets, for our play is played out.

William Thackeray, *Vanity Fair*

All the world is not, of course, a stage, but the crucial ways in which it isn't are not easy to specify.

Erving Goffman, *The Presentation of Self in Everyday Life*

The previous chapter discussed how Realist concerns in the postmodern novel are mediated by representations of history. This chapter will look at how three postmodern novels – *Hawksmoor* by Peter Ackroyd, *The Magus* by John Fowles, and *The White Hotel* by D. M. Thomas – use aspects of theatrical representation. The whole aspect of postmodern performance as analogous to dramatic performance is, indeed, part of the postmodern debate.[1] While drama *per se* will not be the focus here, three aspects of performance will be examined in relation to the novel. First: the novels in this chapter use both textual and textualized performance. That is to say that in some cases the narrative form actually changes to look like a play text (textual), and in others there is a concern with aspects of performance such as role-playing, spectacle, staging, etc., as well as plays which are acted out within the narrative (textualized). A good example of the latter is in *The Magus* where several dramatic performances are undertaken. These are described, however, not presented in the form of a play text. Second: the self-consciousness of these novels, and their delight in flaunting their own artifice means that the very act of representation (of drama, of history, of art) is in itself a performance of representation. Third: the self-consciousness of consciousness of the characters in these novels, also indicates a concern with character (subject) formation. Indeed, the creation of roles (reader, author, novel) is also examined, as is its relation to ideology. These texts, then, question the Realist view that identity is coherent or that there is a definable human essence, through their play with the creation and acting out of roles. Several more detailed comparisons might be made between theatre and the postmodern novel.

The play-fulness of these texts is readily apparent. Not only are they conscious of both the existence of an audience and the vicissitudes of reception, and thus their own manipulative powers, but manipulation is clearly conceived of as a kind of play. Recall, for example, Geoffrey Braithwaite's admonishment of a reader he feels wants to follow him into the lavatory in *Flaubert's Parrot*, or Saleem's confession that he lied about Shiva's death in *Midnight's Children*: "my first out and out lie – although my presentation of the Emergency in the guise of a six-hundred-and-thirty-five-day-long midnight was perhaps excessively romantic, and certainly contradicted the available meteorological data" (Rushdie 1981: 443). Also in this novel, an audience is textualized. Padma, as narratee, listens (she cannot read) as Saleem reads (performs) his story to her, and we "see" her performance as audience. In the theatre of *Midnight's Children*, then, the reader "watches" both actor and audience, and is, because of his/her co-creation of the text, both actor and audience.

Play-fulness is also a questioning of authority on both the level of textual process and that of textual reception. Richard Palmer points out that performance "in drama and in music generally refers to the fact that a script or score must be 'realized' in performance in order to 'be' at all. Of course, a play can be read silently, and a piece of fiction can be 'performed orally'. Performance in both cases is also the interpretive articulation of a script or score" (1977: 19). The indeterminacy of the play text is shared by the novel. The multiplicity of language, and therefore of interpretation, means that every reading is a new *mise-en-scène*. Postmodern novels thus textualize their own indeterminacy. Hawksmoor's comment that "perhaps there is no book in this case" (Ackroyd 1985: 118), and his subsequent invention of an interpretation which is outside his usual role as rational detective is a *mise en abyme*[2] of reading the novel. We see this multiplicity as well in *Star Turn* where Amos' rewriting of the past, culled from films, lies, and fragments of memory, makes history itself a performance. He inverts traditional, serious notions of historical figures, turning them into wild parodies. His re-creation of Goebbels as a schizophrenic who acts out the conflicting personalities of both the Nazi minister of propaganda and Jewish New York taxi driver, Abe Solomons, is a good example of Amos' play with, and performance of, history. *Chekhov's Journey* is perhaps the clearest example of a performance which actually changes history. Mikhail's interpretation of Chekhov, influenced in part by Chekhov's plays, ensures that neither the play texts nor the history texts will ever be the same.

The creation of roles is important here, especially since characters in these novels often have moments of hesitation wherein they distance themselves from their previous performances in order to evaluate and examine them. These moments of analysis also implicate the reader in that, if a character changes roles, the reader is also asked to evaluate how he or she perceives the very idea of character (subject) formation. For instance, the narrator in John Fowles' *The French Lieutenant's Woman* plays numerous parts. He not only addresses the reader on the subject of his/her own self-creation: "You do not even think of your own past as quite real; you dress it up, you gild it or blacken it, censor it, tinker with it . . . fictionalize it, in a word, and put it away on a shelf – your book, your romanced autobiography" (Fowles 1969: 97), he also moves freely from the twentieth to the nineteenth century. He appears as both a passenger in Charles Smithson's Victorian train compartment, and as the "impresario" (Fowles 1969: 462) who leans against the Rossettis' gate and "evidently regards the world as his to possess and use as he likes" (ibid.: 462). Such a tactic raises issues about the function of both narrator and character. By extension, it also problematizes the reader's conception about what constitutes a novel in the first place. As we have seen in *Midnight's Children*, *Star Turn*, *Hawksmoor*, and *Chekhov's Journey*, character (subject) formation is not, as the Realists would have it, unscripted. Ideology, indeed, plays the role of dramatist. The self-conscious manipulation of roles in these novels, then, reminds us that characters as well as readers are constructed in ideology.

Postmodern texts are interrogative in the sense explained by Catherine Belsey in *Critical Practice*. They disrupt "the unity of the reader by discouraging identification with a unified subject of the enunciation" (Belsey 1980: 91). Play and drama are appropriate vehicles for this disruption because they foreground the discontinuity between what Belsey describes as "the 'I' who speaks and the 'I' who is represented in discourse" (1980: 85). Richard Schechner examines this tension in view of theatrical performance in "News, Sex, and Performance Theory:"

> All effective performances share this "not – not not" quality: Olivier is not Hamlet, but also he is not not Hamlet: his performance is between a denial of being another (= I am me) and a denial of not being another (= I am Hamlet). Performer training focuses its techniques not on making one person into another, but on permitting the performer to act inbetween identities; in this sense performing is a paradigm of liminality.
> (Schechner 1983: 189–90)

In the sense that liminality is a threshold and highlights what Schechner calls "inbetweenness" (ibid.: 190), postmodern fiction is essentially liminal, even metaliminal. The postmodern itself is defined in terms of "otherness," even of "notness." As Linda Hutcheon points out in "Beginning to Theorize Postmodernism," definitions of the postmodern are "usually accompanied by a grand flourish of negativized rhetoric: we hear of discontinuity, disruption, dislocation, decentring, indeterminacy and anti-totalization. What all of these words literally do (by their disavowing prefixes, *dis-*, *de-*, *in-*, *anti-*) is incorporate that which they aim to contest – as does, arguably, the term *post*-modernism itself" (1987: 10). We can see this, for example, in *Hawksmoor*. It is *not* a detective novel because it doesn't subscribe unquestioningly to the wiles of the genre. However, it is *not not* a detective novel because it inscribes a superficial layer of recognizable conventions. These novels, then, "act inbetween identities" themselves, and also textualize this in the perform- ances of their characters and examinations of subjectivity.

In *Hawksmoor* characters' identities are confused from the outset. Both Dyer and Hawksmoor think of themselves as distanced from their assigned social roles, and both are aware of creating personae in order to hide from social censure. Dyer has to conceal his religion and his sacrifices, and Hawksmoor must "be seen to be taking some action" (Ackroyd 1985: 195), despite his inability to solve the case. Naming, here, further problematizes identity. Hawksmoor's historical namesake was in fact an architect, a role which in the novel is assigned to Dyer. Dyer builds what are recognizably "Hawksmoor churches," yet he is not Hawksmoor. Detective Hawksmoor is not an architect, although his use of architectural metaphors and his search for the "Universal Architect" creates tension between himself, the "real" Hawksmoor, and Dyer. We can, of course, only know the "real" Hawksmoor through written sources which make him as fictional a creation as Dyer. This fictionalizing is made doubly apparent because of the novel's title, which gives the "real" Hawksmoor a presence in the novel by his very absence from it. Subjectivity can only be defined, here, in/as the tensions between the characters and between the characters' various performances. The novel plays with the Realist notion of unchanging human essence in using, paradoxically, supernatural elements to explain the murders and the relationships between architect Hawksmoor, Dyer, and detective Hawksmoor.

It is interesting that reviewers of the novel comment on how sinister and morbid it is. Jonathan Keates' review in the *Observer* is entitled "Creaking Floorboards" (1985: 27). Geoff Dyer in the *New Statesman* likens it to Nicolas Roeg's film *Don't Look Now* (1985: 34), and Alan Hollinghurst, in the *Times Literary Supplement*, explains that Hawksmoor is "possessed by the spirit of the architect" (1985: 1049). Comments like these reproduced on the dust jacket clearly make terror one of the novel's selling points. It is possible that the perceived terror, though, is not simply the result of the nameless murderer, or the web of suggestions that the spirit of the architect (Dyer or Hawksmoor) is haunting twentieth-century London. The supernatural would presuppose an eternal human essence, but through its concern with performance, *Hawksmoor* discounts the supernatural as a possibility. The construction of identity which can only be perceived in terms of negatives and absences is perhaps the cause of the reviewers' fear and discomfort. In a sense, it would be reassuring if the supernatural were to blame, but this would provide a solution (a name) and thus closure, and as we have seen in its abuse of detective story conventions, *Hawksmoor* also subverts ideas of either solution or closure. Perhaps this, for the reviewers, is the most supernatural element of all.

Hawksmoor addresses the notion of essential human essence in its play with the supernatural. Dyer and Hawksmoor appear to be in a mirror relationship to one another – repetitions of phrases and images, as well as Hawksmoor's discovery of Dyer's notebook seem to enforce this. However, as in the (convex) mirrors they both own, this reflection is a distortion. The mirroring, in fact, points out their differences from one another, the separation between the "I" perceiving and the "other" figured in the mirror. Subjectivity is created in the space between these two "I"s, not as a fixed essence, but as a constantly changing process. The two textual dramas in *Hawksmoor* further exemplify this. Both characters are aware of the distance between their performances and the scripts that society has written for them. It is appropriate, then, that both create themselves as characters in dramas wherein they are forced to behave in socially suitable ways. Both of these dramas are written scripts rather than descriptions of performances. This is important because they thus implicate the reader both as audience and as co-director. As written scripts they act out their own liminality since only through the reader can they be realized.

Nicholas Dyer's play takes place after he has been to the theatre. Here, he sees the audience as part of a masquerade similar to the one appearing on stage:

> So it was . . . that I settled my self down to watch this Assembly with its Amorous Smirks, its A la Mode Grins, its Antick Bows – the World being but a Masquerade, yet one in which the Characters do not know their Parts and must come to the Play-House in order to studdy them.
>
> (Ackroyd 1985: 173–4)

For a while he is drawn into the spectacle, like a child watching "the bright World" (ibid.: 174), until "some Gallants" (ibid.: 174) jump from the pit on to the stage and reduce the play to chaos. This intrusion of "life" into art serves to excite Dyer's ridicule not against the gallants, but against the play which seems to him after the disturbance to be composed of "painted Fictions, wicked Hypocrisies and villainous Customs" (Ackroyd 1985: 174). He forgets the play immediately, dismissing it as trite, but his pleasure in making "Merry among the Fallen" (ibid.: 174) leads him to see his subsequent visit to a raucous tavern with John Vanbrugghe (*sic*) as a play in itself. He calls it *Hospital for Fools*. Here, Dyer mocks the play he has just seen for its play-fulness: "the Sunne was a Round flat shining Disc and the Thunder was a Noise from a Drum or a Pan" (Ackroyd 1985: 175). The conversation that follows revolves around the topic of imitation with Dyer arguing that art should imitate the ancients and Vanbrugghe countering that art should not merely plagiarize but instead should follow nature and "the present Age" (ibid.: 177). This is interesting since the play itself both is and is not an imitation (both of eighteenth-century drama and of the play Dyer has just seen) and in this it imitates the "not – not not" construction of the novel.

In the following chapter of the novel, Hawksmoor too participates in a brief textual play while he is interviewing a tramp about the murders. This performance is in the line of his duty as a police officer, although the exchange between Hawksmoor and the tramp does little to further the investigation. The dialogue is brief and disjointed, and the setting is a small white room with a two-way mirror behind which "Walter took notes and watched this scene" (Ackroyd 1985: 194). As the previous play followed the form of eighteenth-century drama, this one seems modelled on television. Walter, the audience, is watching through the screen of the two-way mirror, and the performance he sees is a simulacrum of an interview since Hawksmoor is, by this point, losing his reason. It is interesting that in both these chapters the textual plays highlight the notion of the performing self even though more elaborate performances take place elsewhere in the chapters. Dyer, prior to his going to the theatre, has to attend the funeral of Yorick Hayes, one of his co-workers and his latest Satanic sacrifice. Hawksmoor, after his interview with the tramp, is dismissed from the case, and has to maintain a semblance of dignity in front of his fellow officers. Under stress, however, he tries to separate his character from the script: "he tried to look at himself as if he were a stranger, so that he might be able to predict his next step" (Ackroyd 1985: 202).

The performative aspect of *Hawksmoor* is clearly an undermining of any stable notion of self. This applies not only to the clearly fictional characters, but also to the "real" historical figure of Nicholas Hawksmoor. It is interesting to note, though, that the illusion of a transcendent essence of self is maintained not only by the injection of the supernatural elements but by an even more familiar ploy. The author's disclaimer, "Any relation to real people, either living or dead, is entirely coincidental. I have employed many sources in the preparation of *Hawksmoor*, but this version of history is my own invention" (Ackroyd 1985: 218), appears at the end of the novel, not, as is usual, at the beginning. This ensures that the illusion of the "real" Nicholas Hawksmoor is a viable one until he is finally exorcized at the end.

In John Fowles' *The Magus*, there is a similar tension between the search for a "real" self and the underlying notion that self is a series of performances. *The Magus* itself has a performance history as a text. Fowles rewrote the 1966 text, and in 1977 published a revised version with an explanatory foreword. In this, he acknowledges some of his "influences," both literary and biographical, and discusses his dissatisfaction with the "haphazard and naively instinctive" (Fowles 1977b: 6) original. In what amounts to an apology, he confesses that even the second version is most attractive to the adolescent mind, and "that it must always substantially remain a novel of adolescence written by a retarded adolescent" (ibid.: 9). Nevertheless, he counters, the novel has an important mission which he describes as an exploration of the antipathy between God and freedom. At the heart of his story, he explains, is the notion that "true freedom lies between each two, never in one alone, and therefore it can never be absolute freedom. All freedom, even the most relative, may be a fiction; but mine, and still today, prefers the other hypothesis" (Fowles 1977b: 10). The author's preface is important here, not for thematic concordance with the text proper, nor for reasons of "influence." Indeed, the preface is, by virtue of its inclusion between the covers, not a separate critical comment, but a part of the text itself. What is interesting about it is what it does with the liminal space it represents. The preface itself is what "lies between each two" editions of *The Magus*. Is it then "true freedom" or is it an assertion of authority that denies the reader a similar right to perform in rewriting the text yet again? The preface is a performance of both authorial humility and control, and the subject is clearly more the rewritten author than the revised text. There are several contradictory impulses here. On one hand, Fowles asserts that the "meaning" of *The Magus* is "whatever reaction it provokes in the reader, and so far as I am concerned there is no given 'right' reaction" (Fowles 1977b: 9). On the other, his reading of the influences on his text, biographical or literary, is not a neutral one. It cannot help but condition the reader's response to the novel.

The performance of the rewritten author (Fowles draws the reader's attention to the difference between this self and the one who wrote the first version) is one which hides the nature of authority that the existence of such a preface must necessarily address. Fowles creates himself as subject to the whims of a (not very mature or intelligent) audience. This novel, he says, which pleases his readers the most, pleases him least. In a sense, the preface is a performance that denies performance – or at least those aspects of it which highlight multiplicity. Paradoxically, Fowles tacitly acknowledges in writing it that the second version of *The Magus* is in itself a performance of the script of the first one. The preface is a curious beginning to a novel whose major concern is with metatheatre and the variety of roles within it. The preface's concerns are those of Realist reading, and this is encouraged through the authority of biographical detail, "influence," and the voice of the author who is penitent for his past "flux." It is an odd beginning to a novel which undermines all of these. Yet in a sense, it is one more layer of the metatheatre because it presents one kind of reader/author relationship among the many the novel explores. In this, Fowles, like Conchis, is playing a "godgame."

The godgame played in *The Magus* consists of a series of frames which are repeatedly established and broken. This framebreaking, as Brian McHale points out, presents us with a series of illusions of "reality:" "Intended to establish an absolute level of reality, it paradoxically *relativizes* reality; intended to provide an ontologically stable foothold, it only destabilizes ontology further" (1987: 197). This is a more than apt description of the effects of Maurice Conchis' "metatheatre" in the novel, a theatre designed "to allow participants to see through their first roles in it" (Fowles 1977b: 408–9). The narrator, Nicholas Urfe, is the subject of a bizarre experiment, the object of which appears to be to make Nicholas accept responsibility for his "true" self. As Conchis explains:

There comes a time in each life like a point of fulcrum. At that time you must accept yourself. It is not any more what you will become. It is what you are and always will be. You are too young to know this. You are still becoming. Not being.

(Fowles 1977b: 109)

At first glance, this speech seems to contradict the very premise of the "metatheatre." It seems, indeed, an adolescent cliché completely opposed to the performance that Nicholas is subjected to. Several of the characters in the drama encourage this (essentially Realist) reading of self. Alison Kelly, Nicholas' lover, exhorts him to talk about "who we really are" (Fowles 1977b: 26), and even uses herself as an example of a static self: "Don't you begin to feel things about yourself you know are you? Are going to be you for ever? That's what I feel" (ibid.: 29). June and Julie, the twins he meets on the island, tell him "we've decided to be ourselves" (ibid.: 326), and Julie responds to Nicholas' "There are so many things I want to know about the real you" with "The real me's a lot less exciting than the imaginary one" (ibid.: 291). In a sense, though, this is the first frame, since it is something Nicholas, who lacks imagination, understands.

From the beginning of the novel, Nicholas is adept at playing roles, usually in order to ensure the success of his sexual conquests: "My 'technique' was to make a show of unpredictability, cynicism, and indifference. Then, like a conjurer with his white rabbit, I produced the solitary heart" (Fowles 1977b: 21). Nevertheless, he is almost romantically involved with the idea of an essential self which he keeps hidden behind his various performances. When his parents are killed in a plane crash, for instance, he feels relief: "I now had no family to trammel what I regarded as my real self" (Fowles 1977b: 16). This apparent concern with a "real" self provides the overt framework for Nicholas' experiences on the Greek island of Phraxos, where he has accepted a job teaching English at a boys' boarding school. His posting provides an excuse to end his affair with Alison which comes as a relief, since her ability to see through his roles makes him uncomfortable. On the island, he tries to assuage his loneliness by writing poetry, but a rare moment of critical insight forces him to the realization that his poems are merely banal. His anger that "evolution could allow such sensitivity and such inadequacy to co-exist in the same mind" (Fowles 1977b: 58), coupled with an apparent bout of syphilis, drive him to the brink of suicide. Shortly after a failed attempt to kill himself, however, "the mysteries" (ibid.: 63) begin.

When Nicholas enters Bourani, he enters a theatre without a recognizable audience and without limits. Conchis eventually explains it as a new kind of drama:

> One in which the conventional separation between actors and audience was abolished. In which the conventional scenic geography, the notions of proscenium, stage, auditorium, were completely discarded. In which continuity of performance, either in time or place, was ignored. And in which the action, the narrative was fluid, with only a point of departure and a fixed point of conclusion. Between those points the participants invent their own drama.
>
> (Fowles 1977b: 404)

On his various visits to Bourani, Nicholas listens to Conchis narrate his life story, events from which are often illustrated by actors and actresses. Nicholas is only briefly "taken in" by the costume dramas that Conchis mounts, although his certainty that they are dramas is constantly undermined by Conchis' refusal to admit to his role as director. Conchis' comment that "We are all actors here, my friend. None of us is what we really are. We all lie some of the time, and some of us all the time" (Fowles 1977b: 404), does not stop Nicholas from trying to ascertain an ultimate reality. Partly, this is fostered by the "theatre" itself. Various scenes are acted out precisely to make Nicholas see through them, to promote the illusion of frame-breaking. This is most consistently achieved through the character of Lily/Julie and her series of roles.

When Conchis' long dead fiancée Lily suddenly appears in the music room at Bourani dressed in pre-First World War costume, Nicholas congratulates himself on his incredulity. Although she plays the part convincingly, he is in no doubt that she is an actress. When the actress steps out of this role into one more closely approximating "reality," Nicholas believes she has left the stage. It is, however, simply another performance, albeit one which is more difficult to detect because it lacks the physical trappings of costume drama. While in this second role, she plays Julie Holmes, Conchis' god-child, a schizophrenic whom he is trying to protect and to cure. Once Nicholas is allowed to see through this, however, he is convinced he has found the "real" Julie. She and June, her twin sister, are, they tell him, actresses employed by Conchis to participate in a movie to be filmed on the island. They, it appears, are only slightly more knowledge-able than is Nicholas about the events at Bourani, and are equally under Conchis' control. His game, Julie explains, is "all about role-playing. How people behave in situations they don't understand" (Fowles 1977b: 340). Here, however, is a situation Nicholas does understand, that of fellow victim. For him, this guarantees the reality of Julie's story. Nevertheless, when Julie tells him her life story, she provides "proof" of her identity such as letters from home, newspaper clippings, and various refer-ences that Nicholas can check. This he does, writing to the twins' mother, as well as to their bank manager in England. The responses he receives satisfy him as to Julie's identity. Various complications that later ensue are explained to Nicholas in terms of Conchis' whims, not in terms of any complicity on the part of the twins. However, this most convincing role also proves to be an illusion. At the end of Conchis' godgame Nicholas is abducted and subjected to a ritual "disintoxication." Here, he is faced with thirteen psychiatrists and psychologists, the apparent perpetrators of the "metatheatre." Among them is Dr Vanessa Maxwell whom Nicholas recognizes as Lily/Julie. This is the last role, and although Nicholas discovers that it is yet another performance, he cannot now discover the "truth," even though he is allowed to meet the twins' real mother. On her, he heaps his anger that the "metatheatre" is anti-mimetic.

Each of these roles leads Nicholas closer to what he thinks is "reality," yet each is an undercutting of the notion of an absolute "reality." Each is an affirmation of relativity. Nicholas' response to this is to adopt the role of Realist reader. Back in London he seeks correspondence between the events at Bourani and "reality." Conchis has warned him that "all here is artifice" (Fowles, 1977b: 406), but Nicholas cannot accept that Conchis' masque is neither mimetic nor expressive (in the traditional interpretive senses).

In "News, Sex, and Performance Theory," Richard Schechner comments on the simultaneously perceived levels of meta-performance, and his explanation of the various "modes of seeing" is appropriate to *The Magus* as a text which both performs and thematizes performance:

> A person sees the event; he sees himself; he sees himself seeing the event; he sees himself seeing others who are seeing the event and who, maybe, see themselves seeing the event. Thus there is the performance, the performers, the spectators; and the spectator of spectators; and the self-seeing-self that can be performer or spectator or spectator of spectators.
>
> (Schechner, 1983: 191)

For the reader, the variety of roles and perceptions of roles, as well as the layering of frames, makes the entire novel a meta-theatrical event. We can see this not only in the roles the characters play, but also in the novel's structure and narrative technique. The chapters themselves are a series of frames like the frames that Nicholas encounters in the novel. The first of the author-figures in *The Magus*, John Fowles, provides, in his foreword, a framework for reading which the novel itself undercuts. This is clear from Nicholas' failure to explain his experiences at Bourani through "real" referents or biographical details. Since Fowles, of course, is the "real" author, albeit a performing one, his "prologue" sets the stage for the mixture of fiction and "reality" which is to follow. The first chapter of the novel proper presents a world which is verisimilar, and the illusion is maintained by having fictional characters live in the "real" London. When, in the second chapter, "the mysteries" begin, the reader is encouraged to "identify" with Nicholas as the only constant. Yet this too is made problematic because of the fluidity of characters' roles, as well as by the repetitions of and insistence on ideas about acting, staging, costumes, and perform-ances. Nicholas is, after all, also a character in the metatheatre. In the final chapter, Nicholas arrives back in London. The apparent end of Conchis' masque proves to have been yet another performance, however, and the theatre continues even off the delineated "stage" at Bourani. Nicholas is still subjected to stage-managed moments even in the safety of his own familiar "reality." Appropriately enough, then, this last chapter is a frame with only three sides, giving the illusion that the theatre can spill out into the reader's world as well.

The reader is not only implicated in the performance, reader and author roles are also acted out within the novel. When Conchis, as author-figure, creates an alternate world at Bourani, Nicholas reads it as manipulative and abusive because it is outside the realm of his comprehension. He interprets Conchis' actions as a detective in a detective fiction would interpret evidence: there is the assumption that there is a "normal" and universal mode of behavior, otherwise the anomaly, or clue, would never be found. As Nicholas himself finally realizes, "to view life as a detective story, as something that could be deduced, hunted and arrested, was no more realistic (let alone poetic) than to view the detective story as the most important literary genre, instead of what it really was, one of the least" (Fowles 1977b: 552). However, when Nicholas takes on the role of magus, as narrator of the novel, he turns precisely the same kind of abuse on the reader as that which he suffered in Conchis' hands. The authority of the narrative voice is repeatedly asserted and denied, expectations are created and destroyed, the same frames are used on the reader as were used on Nicholas as reader, and solutions to the mysteries are never revealed. The novel's open ending is a good example of this play with the reader since it parallels Nicholas' experience of Conchis' theatre to the reader's experience with *The Magus* in his/her own world. The ending is a parodic reference to Keats' "Ode on a Grecian Urn:"

> She is silent, she will never speak, never forgive, never reach a hand, never leave this frozen present tense. All waits, suspended. Suspend the autumn trees, the autumn sky, anonymous people. A blackbird, poor fool, sings out of season from the willows by the lake. A flight of pigeons over the houses; fragments of freedom, hazard, an anagram made flesh. And somewhere the stinging smell of burning leaves.
>
> (Fowles 1977b: 656)

This, like the Keats poem it refers to, is an eternal liminal space, and as such is a confirmation of artifice. The ending, therefore, sends conflicting messages to the reader. On one hand, it implicates the reader as the ultimate performer since only she or he can fill in the phenomenological gaps in this frozen scene. On the other, however, the flaunting of the novel as artifice precludes the reader's making judgements about what "really" happened to Nicholas and Alison, and thus from allowing the theatre to spill over the boundaries of the novel. Nicholas and Alison, after all, do not exist outside the realm of *The Magus*. This is the triumph of metatheatre over Realist reading, in other words, because it insists that there are *only* levels of performance and illusions of "reality."

The levels of performance which question the notion of essential subjectivity are equally apparent in D. M. Thomas' *The White Hotel*. In this novel, Lisa Erdman, a minor opera singer, seeks analytic help from "Sigmund Freud" because of the possible psychological causes of severe pains in her left breast and pelvic region, and a chronic respiratory condition. During the course of her analysis she writes a lengthy poem between the staves of a score of *Don Giovanni* as well as a prose elaboration of the same scenes described in the poem. Both are, as "Freud" describes them, "an extreme of libidinous phantasy combined with an extreme of morbidity. It is as if Venus looked in the mirror and saw the face of Medusa" (Thomas 1981: 13). Her writings provide the basis for Lisa's analysis, although, as we later discover, various associations which she makes based on these two phantasies hide, rather than reveal, her past. In his analysis of Lisa, whom he calls "Frau Anna G." in his case study, "Freud" finds an example of a "*universal* struggle between the life instinct and the death instinct" (Thomas 1981: 117), one of whose manifestations is "an irrational compulsion to repeat" (ibid.: 118). The reason for this, he speculates (as did Freud himself in *Beyond the Pleasure Principle* (1920: 36), might be found in the conservatism of human instincts: "Might it not therefore be that all living things are in mourning for the inorganic state, the original condition from which they have by accident emerged?" (Thomas 1981: 117). "Freud"'s analysis of Lisa is, of course, based on an examination of her past traumas, repetitions of whose imagery, both in and out of analysis, bring on recurrences of her acute physical discomforts. The structure of the text itself seems to enforce this since in each of its seven parts images are vividly repeated. This puts the reader in the same position as both "Freud" and Lisa since the reader too is asked to read retrospectively because of the novel's compulsion to repeat.

For "Freud" there is certainly an essential subjectivity which is the result of universal instinctual phenomena. Lisa's repeated symptoms are, for "Freud," a re-enactment of a past event of which she is both aware and unaware. Her psyche is producing clues to the true nature of this past event, and they are, in a sense, in a mimetic relationship to it:

> What she had in her consciousness was only a secret and not a foreign body. She both knew and did not know. In a sense, too, her mind was attempting to tell us what was wrong; for the repressed idea creates its own apt symbol. The psyche of an hysteric is like a child who has a secret, which no one must know, but everyone must guess. And so he must make it easier by scattering clues. Clearly the child in Frau Anna's mind was telling us to look at her breast and her ovary; and precisely the left breast and ovary, for the unconscious is a precise and even pedantic symbolist.
>
> (Thomas 1981: 91)

The unconscious, for "Freud," is not a culturally produced construct which is mediated by language. Instead, it is the innate, essential, coherent self. As a subject, Lisa *is* her instinctual life to which, in turn, she is subjected. This is further stressed in "Freud"'s case history by his authoritative appeal to transcultural universals in his explanation of Lisa's hysteria. Such comments as: "childhood masturbation (an almost universal phenomenon)" (Thomas 1981: 92); "a hearty, jovial man, as uncles are supposed to be" (ibid.: 86); "Train journeys are themselves dreams of death" (ibid.: 95); and "Every young girl, when she reaches the Oedipal stage, begins to nurse destructive impulses towards her mother" (ibid.: 125), all reinforce the "Freudian" (and Freudian) conception of essential subjectivity. However, both "Freud"'s and Freud's authority on both the coherent individual subject and the repetition compulsion is called into question by the roles Lisa plays throughout the novel, as well as by her telepathy, which points to her symptoms as foreshadowing an event, rather than repeating one.

The title of the first chapter, "Don Giovanni," signals the novel's concern with performance as does Lisa's role as Tatiana in *Eugene Onegin*. Both these intertexts juxtapose *Eros* and *Thanatos*, the proximity of which "Freud" notes in Lisa's past, but whose importance becomes horrifyingly clear in the manner of her death: she is raped with a bayonet on top of a "sea of bodies covered in blood" (Thomas 1981: 217) at Babi Yar. Lisa rewrites both these operas making herself their subject, and thus pointing to her own life as a series of roles. In the pornographic poem written as an alternative libretto to *Don Giovanni*, Lisa dramatizes herself as a split subject. She is "split open" (Thomas 1981: 20), a "broken woman" (ibid.: 20), "torn" (ibid.: 23), and in a dream her "breast was sheared away" (ibid.: 24). At the end of her poem, she writes of her "otherness:" "it was good/ to feel a part of me was someone else,/ no one was selfish in the white hotel" (Thomas 1981: 30). In his analysis of this phantasy, "Freud" tries to convince Lisa that its various parts are aspects of her coherent identity. He is convinced that her phantasy "might teach us everything, if we were only in a position to make everything out" (Thomas 1981: 105). Lisa's response, however, is to take on other roles in her explanation of her phantasy, some of which, as we later discover, are conscious fictions. Her poem, and the subsequent elaboration of it in prose are, she says, "just my life" (Thomas 1981: 111). If her "Don Giovanni" phantasies are a mirror of Lisa's life, they clearly point out the difference between the "I" writing and the "I" written. Ironically, "Freud" underlines this difference when he registers surprise at her knowledge of pornographic language: "I was astonished where she had learned such terms, for she had not, to my knowledge, frequented the places where they were spoken" (Thomas 1981: 104). Like the mirror image, the novel's play with time also indicates the "inbetweenness" of Lisa's identity. In the "Prologue" to the novel, "Hans Sachs" comments on Lisa's phantasies which remind him of "Eden before the Fall – not that love and death did not happen there, but there was no *time* in which they could have a meaning" (Thomas 1981: 15). Similarly, there is no time in Lisa's phantasies in which "meaning" can be ascertained by "Freud." They are certainly connected with her past, but they also foreshadow her future, and thus are less fantastic than frightening. This liminality, signalled in terms of time, is an equally appropriate signal of Lisa's liminal identity, composed as it is by a series of time-less roles.

Another aspect of her liminal identity becomes clear when we examine Lisa's role as Tatiana, one which she re-enacts when she replies to Victor's proposal of marriage. Her apparent fear of physical intimacy causes "Freud" to suggest that she has latent homosexual tendencies, and her apparent bisexuality is a further reminder of her acting inbetween identities. It is appropriate, then, that she should choose to respond to Victor's proposal by refashioning the letter scene from *Eugene Onegin*, since his proposal of marriage throws her into a fit of indecision, and so she can only respond to him as a performer. Indeed, she allows the "rhymes to lead her to a correct decision" (Thomas 1981: 182). This poem, like the "Don Giovanni" one, reveals Lisa's "otherness." She both is and is not Tatiana, and she highlights her sense of indeterminacy further in adding that she is "A still naive/Young girl in wrinkled flesh" (Thomas 1981: 184) with a voice "Harsh as the raven/Who was *almost* a nightingale" (ibid.: 184).

It is interesting that this is the only performance of Tatiana, or of any of her operatic roles, we "see" Lisa give, since the most consistent aspect of performance in *The White Hotel* is rehearsal. A rehearsal both is and is not a performance, yet in some senses it is *more* performative than the opening night, which is "the real thing." The rehearsal is a constant looking forward to a performance which is in itself a looking back to rehearsal. In "The Gastein Journal," the prose version of "Don Giovanni," Lisa is learning and rehearsing a Verdi opera on the train. When, at the end of his case history, "Freud" tells of meeting "Anna" a year after the termination of her analysis, she is on her way to a rehearsal. "Freud," significantly, does not see her perform, pleading a "lack of appreciation of modern music" (Thomas 1981: 129). In "The Health Resort" she is again rehearsing on a train, this time for the role of Tatiana as a replacement for a singer who has been injured in a fall. Although we "see" Lisa rehearsing for her role on the stage at La Scala, we do not "see" her performance.

The textual insistence on rehearsal rather than performance is borne out in the structure of the text. "Freud" sees Lisa's compulsion to repeat as evidence of traumas in her past. However, Lisa's clairvoyance, which is acknowledged by "Freud," shows that the repetitions are rehearsals not re-enactments. She is foreseeing her death at Babi Yar whose terrifying circumstances are the culmination, the performance, as it were, of the images which recur throughout the novel. In this sense, we can see the structure of the novel both as a five-act tragedy with prologue and epilogue, and as a series of rehearsals leading up to Lisa's death in "The Health Resort." The "Prologue," which includes letters written by and to "Freud," provides program notes which set the stage for the circumstances of the following two chapters. It also includes a "viewer discretion is advised" clause in "Freud"'s letter to the Secretary General of the Goethe Committee:

> I hope you will not be alarmed by the obscene expressions scattered throughout her poor verses, nor by the somewhat less offensive, but still pornographic, material in the expansion of her phantasy. It should be borne in mind that (a) their author was suffering from a severe sexual hysteria, and (b) the compositions belong to the realm of science, where the principle of *nihil humanum* is universally accepted and applied; and not least by the poet who advised his readers not to fear or turn away from "what, unknown or neglected by men, walks in the night through the labyrinth of the heart".
>
> (Thomas 1981: 15)

The concluding chapter, "The Camp," takes place after Lisa's death. The camp is a transitional place on the way to what appears to be an Edenic life after death. The imagery from the preceding chapters is repeated here, and, like the images, characters are resurrected from Lisa's past. The chapter becomes, therefore, a curtain call where characters and images take their last bows.

In "Presence and Play" Michel Benamou writes that "Performance, the unifying mode of the postmodern, is now what matters" (1977: 3). It is a unity born out of multiplicity, however, because the performative metaphor problematizes Realist ideas of representation and subjectivity by foregrounding liminality and indeterminacy. As we have seen, performance is not just thematized or textualized within the postmodern novel, the novel itself performs and thus implicates the reader in its theatre. The following chapter will examine how film and visual art, also performative media, engage the reader in a further play with Realist conventions.

Chapter four

Un-mastering masterful images

The previous chapters have examined the various devices which postmodern texts use to play with Realist techniques. This chapter will examine three novels which mediate Realist conventions through visual art and film. In *Lanark*, by Alasdair Gray, *Midnight's Children* by Salman Rushdie, and *Daniel Martin* by John Fowles, the presentation and subversion of Realist conventions is explored in the tension between visual and verbal images. In *Lanark*, these visual images are both textual (the author's illustrations accompany the text) and textualized (the protagonist, Duncan Thaw, creates paintings which are described verbally). In *Midnight's Children*, Saleem Sinai uses cinematic language and images to give an illusion of continuity and coherence, and in *Daniel Martin*, Daniel pits film and novel against one another in order to see which one will best communicate his "real" self.

In *Lanark*, the tyranny of the visual image as a mimetic device is paralleled in the exploration of structures of power. In the other two novels, the authority of the visual image is ideologically produced, particularly since, in these novels, the image is seen to be reproduced unmediated by technology or ideology. What is seen is believed, and both narrators try to manipulate their readers into believing that the references to visual images are in themselves visual, not words on a page.

Lanark opens in the surrealistic, sunless city of Unthank where aleatory bureaucracy and strange diseases (dragon skin, mouths, softs, twittering rigor) plague the citizens. The character Lanark has been deposited in Unthank, but the circumstances of his arrival elude him. He has no memory of his past, but he does remember sunlight, and he spends most of his time searching for it. A patch of scaly skin which grows on his elbow eventually covers his arm, turning it into a dragon's claw and, understandably distressed, he begins to seek a method of escape from Unthank. This appears in the form of a giant, disembodied mouth which appears one day on the ground in front of him. It invites him to jump in and he does. When he comes to, he finds himself in the Institute, a place where the diseased are sometimes cured, but more often are used in sinister ways to provide food and fuel for this subterranean hospital. Disgusted by what he discovers, Lanark leaves the Institute, but before he does, he requests information about his past and is obliged by an oracle.

The oracle's story is of Duncan Thaw, Lanark's past self, growing up in Glasgow during and after the Second World War. He is an introspective, selfish child who is debilitated by bizarre fantasies, eczema, and asthma. Although a poor student, he has a talent for drawing and is eventually admitted to the Glasgow Art School. Thaw is unable to finish any of his works, and his frustration at the restrictions imposed on him by the school leads to serious bouts of asthma which confine him to a hospital bed. In hospital, he meets a minister who commissions Thaw to paint a mural on the ceiling of his parish church. Like all Thaw's projects, however, the mural is unfinished, and is too unorthodox for the parishioners to wish it completed. Without employment or money, Thaw's mental and physical health decline, and he finally commits suicide.

In the final section of the novel, Lanark leaves the Institute and returns to Unthank. Conditions there have significantly deteriorated – food supplies have been cut off and poison has been leaked into the water. Lanark is elected to fly to Provan, a neighboring city, to a general assembly of council states, where he is to plead for improvements. However, the corporate conglomeration, "the creature," (Gray 1981: 371) which runs Unthank, has already decided to destroy it, and Lanark is powerless to avert catastrophe. He returns to Unthank, which is already burning and flooding, and dies at the moment the novel ends.

Lanark's primary concern is with structures of power, from familial, governmental, and corporate control, to the manipulation of the reader and the character, Lanark, by the very structure of the text. This is based on connections made between minute, and superficially unimportant, details of plot and language. While detail is one of the Realist conventions, here it has more to do with creating a resemblance to the appearance of formal structure than truth to life. This is clear from the epigraph taken from *Waiting for Godot* (Beckett 1977: 11) which functions as a *mise en abyme* of the novel's structural play with Realism in announcing both an event and its non-performance:

Vladimir: Suppose we repented?
Estragon: Repented what?
Vladimir: Oh . . . (*he reflects*) We wouldn't have to go into the details.

(Gray 1981: i)

The importance of detail as a structural device is signalled to the reader by the illustrated title pages, the Epilogue, and the entire fantasy world of Unthank. As we discover, Unthank is the world of "after death," and as such is a fantasy since the concept of "after death" only exists linguistically (Hutcheon 1984: 98). As Brian Aldiss puts it, it is a world where "reality is about as reliable as a Salvador Dali Watch."[1] Interestingly, it is metaphor, a detail of language, which signals to the reader that this is a fantasy world. When Lanark tells his associate Sludden, "I'm looking for daylight" (Gray 1981: 4), the reader's immediate response (not knowing Unthank's blackness) is to invest the phrase with metaphor. Sludden's response, though, "Go on. You couldn't discuss it with many people, but I've thought things out" (ibid.:5), casts doubt on this first interpretation. It soon becomes clear that words such as "sun," "day," "daylight," and "dawn," which have referents in the reader's world, have none in Unthank, but this does not make them metaphorical. Lanark is, in fact, looking for a real light in the otherwise black sky.

If words from the reader's "reality" make no sense in Unthank, the reverse is also true. Familiar words are invested with meanings which are often unclear to both Lanark and the reader. Diseases common in Unthank, for example, are all named with words with which the reader is perhaps familiar, but whose meaning cannot be gleaned from his or her understanding of them. Metaphor, here, becomes frighteningly literal as we discover that diseases are embodiments of colloquial descriptions of personality. Lanark develops dragon skin, which is the result of his emotional frigidity. A doctor at the Institute explains:

> many people are afraid of the cold and try to keep more heat than they give, they stop the heat from leaving through an organ or limb, and the stopped heat forges the surface into hard insulating armour. . . . And since men feel the heat they receive more than the heat they create the armour makes the remaining human parts feel colder. So do they strip it off? Seldom. . . . So someone may start off by limiting only his affections or lust or intelligence, and eventually heart, genitals, brain, hands and skin are crusted over.
>
> (Gray 1981: 68)

Similarly, "mouths" are developed by "leeches" as one character explains: "But they drove even Sludden away in the end (the mouths did), because as I grew worse I needed him more and he didn't like that" (ibid.: 360). Severe, rigid characters develop "twittering rigor," as a brigadier tells Lanark: "I grew to be nine feet tall and as brittle as glass. I could exert fantastic pressure vertically, upward or downward, but the slightest sideways blow would have cracked me open. We do crack, you know, in the army" (Gray 1981: 54).

Chronology in Unthank is also different from that of our experience; indeed, it is Dali-esque, as we discover, because time is under government control. Metaphor here too becomes literal. Since money is scarce, it is actually possible to "live on borrowed time." Government advertizements in Greater Unthank proclaim that time really is money: "A home is money. Money is time. Buy time for your family from the Quantum Chronological. (They'll love you for it)" (Gray, 1981: 432); "Money is time. Time is life. Buy life for your family from the Quantum Interminable. (They'll love you for it)" (ibid.: 454). Lanark's flight to Provan in a creature which is half bird, half plane, is paid for with a credit card which allows the vehicle to draw energy from the passenger's future, a luxury which accounts in part for Lanark's rapid aging.

Another aspect of the novel's play with time is that the internal chronology of Lanark is influenced by the external structure of the novel. Even the most cursory glance at the table of contents must, at the very least, make the reader aware of his or her normal expectations of a novel's structure. *Lanark* begins with Book Three, followed by the Prologue, Book One, Book Two, and Book Four, with the Epilogue appearing four chapters before the end of the novel. As Nastler, the author-figure whom Lanark meets in the Epilogue, points out, however, it is not unusual for a novel to begin *in medias res*: "I want *Lanark* to be read in one order but eventually thought of in another. It's an old device. Homer, Virgil, Milton, and Scott Fitzgerald used it" (Gray 1981: 483). While the device may be a familiar one, calling attention to it through the very numbering of the books is an innovation. It is a signal to the reader to look for similar structural systems in the novel, particularly because the book's structural chronology influences that of both Glasgow and Unthank. It is not surprising when a character tells Lanark: "We don't bother much with time now" (Gray 1981: 18), nor that Thaw is cautioned: "None of the clocks in this house can be relied upon, least of all the ones that go" (ibid.: 273). The repeated allusions to time, then, call attention to the structure, and this structure, in turn, dictates the nature of time within the world of the novel.

This play with metaphor, which emphasizes the slippery multiplicity of language, also seems initially to create a distance between the fantasy world of Unthank and the "real" one of Glasgow. However, the Glasgow chapters contain Scots words, and while Realist convention would assume that this use of language captures the true flavor of the locale, it in fact distances the reader unfamiliar with Scots just as much as do the non-referential words in Unthank. Words such as "dauner" (walk or stroll), "keeked" (peeked), and "midden-rakers" (garbage pickers) make Glasgow as distant and as fictional a world as Unthank.

This authoritative control through, at first, seemingly Realist detail is equally apparent in the five extraordinarily complex title pages illustrated with line drawings by the author. These drawings have two prose equivalents: the paintings created by Duncan Thaw and described in prose, and the Epilogue which, because of its complex typography, imitates in prose images what the title pages do in visual ones.

The illustrated title pages are by no means parading as photographs; they are, in fact, closer to cartoons. Yet they exert

Figure 1

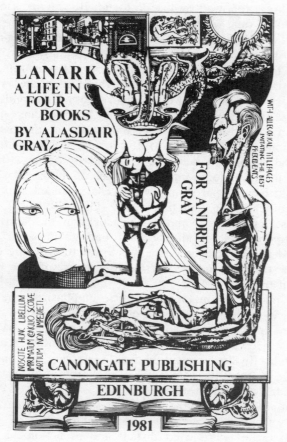

tremendous control in shaping the way the reader reads the text. Like the prose, they are structured with minute detail, and they point to many significant features of the novel. The frontispiece (Figure 1), containing a drawing of a drawing drawing itself (both of which emanate from an open book which is resting on three other open books) signals the auto-referential structure of the novel. It also anticipates, in form and content, the overtly self-conscious Epilogue. The epilogue is described as a room as well as a chapter and, just inside the door of the Epilogue room are paintings which reflect the room. These signal the self-conscious-

Figure 2

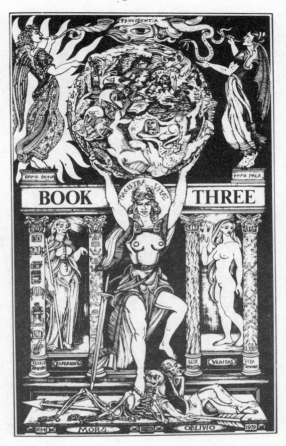

ness of the ensuing chapter, just as the frontispiece, just inside the "door" of *Lanark*, signals the self-consciousness of the novel. The title pages also point to parodic intertexts which give the novel its particular ontological status. The frontispiece, in fact, describes the illustrations as "allegorical . . . imitating the best precedents." The most significant of these intertexts is the title page to Hobbes' *Leviathan*, from which we can see again both the thematized and structural concern with power. Indeed, the very process of gaining power can be seen through the references to Hobbes' sovereign figure in the title pages to *Lanark*: in the

Figure 3

frontispiece to the novel, is the tail of a leviathan; in the title
page to Book Three (Figure 2), this has become a complete
whale within the globe that the *Magistra Vitae* holds in her hands;
the illustration to Book One (Figure 3) shows a fierce whale with
its mouth open waiting to devour an approaching ship. Also in
this title page is half of Hobbes' sovereign figure wreathed in
clouds. His sword appears to be cutting through the darkness, but
from his mouth emanates a shaft of light or lightning which also
appears to threaten the ship in the foreground. By the title page
to Book Four (Figure 5), the sovereign figure reigns over a

Figure 4

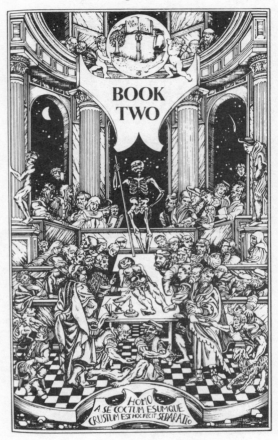

detailed drawing of a city with both "Persuasion" and "Force,"
and the drawings at the bottom of the illustration show the
Althusserian Ideological State Apparatuses of control, persuasion, and regimentation: the army, war, an assembly line, and
education.

Nowhere in the novel is the concern with power more overt
than in the title pages and their authoritative manipulation of the
reader. Like the phenomenon of the "movie of the book" (or
worse, the mini-series), these images make abstractions concrete,
and in this way encourage a Realist reading of the relationship

107

Figure 5

between the visual images and the prose. They create the illusion of one-to-one correspondence, as though the images capture an external "reality" which is then mirrored in prose. Or that, juxtaposed with the prose, the illustrations become the "reality" that language re-presents. We can see this in the chronology which is enforced in the title pages as opposed to the structural chronology of the novel. In each of the first three illustrations is a Greek column. Classical sculptors developed column ornaments in the order of Doric, Ionic, Corinthian. Even though the books are ordered Three, One, and Two, Book One has Doric, Book Two Ionic (Figure 4), and Book Three, Corinthian columns).

An interesting difference between the visual and linguistic images in the text is in the use of fantasy. In Unthank, as we have seen, fantasy is created through literalized metaphor. However, when, as in the title page to Book Three, fantastic creations – the continent of Melancholia, Atlantis, or mermaids – are literalized in images, they are no longer abstractions. They have a single meaning, a truth, which is then imposed on the prose.

In creating his own paintings, Duncan Thaw seems initially to fall into the sort of mimetic trap imposed by the authority of the text's illustrations. Preparing for a painting of the Last Supper, he spends his time "collecting" faces and expressions appropriate to the disciples. Since the disciples were chosen "from labourers and clerks" (Gray 1981: 245), he seeks out labourers and clerks on the underground railway. The face of Jesus, however, is more difficult. Eventually, he finds the expression he wants in a fifteenth-century Flemish trinity, but cannot reproduce it because "nobody can paint an expression that is not potentially their own and this face was beyond him" (Gray 1981: 246). Similarly, for a painting of Blackhill locks, he studies their history and statistics. However, his paintings play with different ways of seeing. Since he cannot reproduce the face of Christ, he decides "to imagine the supper as Jesus would see it from the head of the table. On each side of the board the disciples, anxious, hopeful, doubting, delighted, hungry, replete, were craning and leaning for a glimpse of the viewer's face. The only visible part of Jesus was his hands on the tablecloth" (Gray 1981: 246). Thaw's painting of the locks has an equally imaginative perspective: "He painted them as they would appear to a giant lying on his side, with eyes more than a hundred feet apart and tilted at an angle of forty five degrees" (ibid.: 279). Thaw is clearly not one who believes in the Realist reading position.

Language, of course, allows for greater abstraction than do visual images, and Thaw's capacity for abstract thought is established early in the novel when, as a school-child, he tries to write a story about a boy who hears colors. Responses to his imagination are often derogatory. A fellow student's reaction to his Last Supper, for example, is quite different from what the reader might have expected from the narrative descriptions of it:

"Duncan, do you enjoy drawing those unpleasant people? Or does your picture shock you as much as us?" (Gray 1981: 246). However, the different "readings" of his paintings add to the novel's emphasis on multiple perspectives. It is clear that Thaw recognizes a variety of ways of seeing from his very first drawing:

> Duncan Thaw drew a blue line along the top of a sheet of paper and a brown line along the bottom. He drew a giant with a captured princess running along the brown line, and since he couldn't draw the princess lovely enough he showed the giant holding a sack. The princess was in the sack.
>
> (Gray 1981: 121)

However, when his father asks him to explain his drawing, Thaw re-interprets it as "a miller running to the mill with a bag of corn" (ibid.: 121). Thaw's art teacher criticizes him for sketching a tiny seashell with harsh black lines and all the delicacy of a machine but, once again, he relies on viewing it from a different angle: "the shell only seems delicate and simple because it's smaller than we are. To the fish inside, it was a suit of armour, a house, a moving fortress" (Gray 1981: 229).

Thaw's *magnum opus*, a mural depicting the six days of creation which he is commissioned to paint on the ceiling of a local parish church, is perhaps the best example of multiple perspectives. Indeed, the process of painting it is an arduous one, partly because Thaw envisions such a multitude of possibilities that he cannot limit himself to a single, finished work. He is constantly re-interpreting and re-working every image that he paints. The sketches he makes for the church are unorthodox, but he justifies them by explaining that he wants to represent various notions of the creation, and as the mural takes shape, it is described in detail. Yet, other characters who "see" the mural call into question what the reader has "seen." Like Thaw's previous paintings, this one is criticized for its distortion of the "norm" – the face of God is frightening to some and enigmatic to others, and the ruby skin color of Adam and Eve is seen as blasphemous. An art critic, however, explains that the mural invites different interpretations precisely because it is not definable by any particular school or style:

> Of course it will be almost impossible for me to criticize it. It

isn't cubist or expressionist or surrealist, it isn't academic or kitchen sink or even naive. It's a bit like Puvis de Chavannes, but who nowadays knows Puvis de Chavannes? I'm afraid you're going to pay the penalty of being outside the mainstreams of development.

(Gray 1981: 328)

The mural cannot be conceptualized or categorized and thus cannot be accorded a single, authoritative meaning.

The final level of auto-representation, the Epilogue, is certainly the most fascinating. It is in this overtly self-conscious chapter that Lanark meets the author-figure, Nastler. Although the Epilogue appears four chapters *before* the end of the novel, it serves, we are told, "the office of an introduction to the work as a whole" (Gray 1981: 499). Nastler explains to Lanark that it is thus far too important to be placed after the end of the novel:

Though not essential to the plot it provides some comic distraction at a moment when the narrative sorely needs it. And it lets me offer some fine sentiments which I could hardly trust to a mere character. And it contains critical notes which will save research scholars years of toil. In fact my epilogue is so essential that I am working on it with nearly a quarter of the book still unwritten. I am working on it here, just now, in this conversation. But you have had to reach this room by passing through several chapters I haven't clearly imagined yet, so you know details of the story which I don't.

(Gray 1981: 483)

What is remarkable about this statement is not just the revelation of the character's autonomy; repeated references to Flann O'Brien indicate that this is not an unprecedented device. The Epilogue gives the illusion that the reader has been allowed to co-create parts of the novel which Nastler has not written, but which the reader has read. The chapter is, in fact, being created through the very process of reading as is pointedly revealed by the lines which both Lanark and the reader read:

Much of it seemed to be dialogue but Lanark's eye was caught by a sentence in italics which said: *Much of it seemed to be dialogue but Lanark's eye was caught by a sentence in italics which said.*

(Gray 1981: 481)

The Epilogue presents the reader with a tremendous amount of information. As well as commenting on the processes of reading and writing, Nastler and Lanark, in the narrative, discuss the novel's ending, and debate the character's autonomy. As a justification for Lanark's eventual failure, Nastler cites a list of literary precedents – *The Odyssey, The Aeneid, Don Quixote, The Bible, Paradise Lost* – in which heroes fail. Although Lanark wants a happy ending, Nastler points out the impossibility of this in an assertion of authorial control: "If I give you an ending like that I will be like ten thousand other cheap illusionists! I would be as bad as the late H.G. Wells! I would be worse than Goethe. Nobody who knows a thing about life or politics will believe me for a minute" (Gray 1981: 492).

Outside the narrative are other pieces of information which force the reader to make a conscious decision about how his or her reading will proceed. In the very appearance of the pages, the Epilogue simulates in print what the title pages do in images. The running titles briefly summarize what is happening in the narrative. For example: "The Conjuror Imagines How to Make us All Happy" (Gray 1981: 490–1); "Grotesque Gafuffles, Fine Sentiments And Happy Endings" (ibid.: 494–5). In the footnotes, a literal-minded editor makes often useless comments on the text such as: "But the fact remains that the plots of the Thaw and Lanark sections are independent of each other and cemented by typographical contrivances rather than formal necessity. A possible explanation is that the author thinks a heavy book will make a bigger splash than two light ones" (Gray 1981: 493).

The most interesting part of the Epilogue, however, is the marginalia where an "Index of Plagiarisms" charts the types and degrees of literary theft that have occurred throughout the novel:

There are three kinds of literary theft in this book: *BLOCK PLAGIARISM*, where someone else's work is printed as a distinct typographical unit, *IMBEDDED PLAGIARISM*, where stolen words are concealed within the body of the narrative, and *DIFFUSE PLAGIARISM*, where scenery, characters, actions or novel ideas have been stolen without the original words describing them. To save space these will be referred to hereafter as Blockplag, Implag, and Difplag.

(Gray 1981: 485)

Despite the obvious play here, the plags initially promote the same kind of reading as do the title pages. However, while they invite reading for correspondence, it is clear that the purpose of these plags is sheer delight in the structure created by retrospective reading, especially since the applicability of the plags is often specious. It is easy to see, for example, the connection between the Implag "I will rise with my flaming hair and eat men like air" (Gray 1981: 94), and the lines from Sylvia Plath's "Lady Lazarus": "I rise with my red hair/And I eat men like air" (ibid.: 495). Other plags are more diffuse, and many are to minute, apparently unimportant details. The reference to T. S. Eliot, for example, is not, as one might expect, to plagiarism in general. Rather, it is to a single, rather innocuous line: " 'I'm something commonplace that keeps getting hurt' is a drab Difplag of the 'notion of some infinitely gentle,/Infinitely suffering thing' in *Preludes*" (Gray 1981: 487–8). Finally, emphasizing the novel's structural self-consciousness, some of the plags refer only to themselves. The reference to Black Angus, for example, tells the reader to "See Macneacail, Aonghas" (Gray 1981: 486). Macneacail, Aonghas refers the reader to "Nicholson, Angus" (ibid.: 493), which refers back to Black Angus.

If there were by this point any doubt in the reader's mind about the subversion of Realist techniques, the Index of Plagiarisms points to the ultimate open ending. References are made to plagiarisms in Chapters forty-five to fifty, which is only remarkable once the reader discovers that the novel ends at Chapter forty-four. In order to figure this out, however, the reader has to read in precisely the way which is undermined by the discovery of these absent chapters. He or she has to read for correspondence as he or she is encouraged to do by the illustrated title pages. In the plags to these missing chapters, real authors and texts are combined with fantastic events in chapters which are themselves, of course, fictions. When they are put in order by chapter and paragraph, the plags seem to depict the story of a cosmic battle which continues past the end of *Lanark* (see Appendix, pp. 126–7). The references are so abstract, however, that they could certainly be read in a variety of ways. Like Thaw's paintings, they emphasize multiplicity.

Paradoxically, however, while the novel undermines authority – the corruptibility of structures of power is the subject of the novel's plot – it does so in an extremely authoritarian way. In the last chapters Lanark, despite his apparent autonomy, is frequently subjected to manipulation to the point that he loses control of his language:

I'll play it by ear, I'll play it hot, gelid, dirty, depending on how he deals the deck. I'll cash every one of them in my suit and then some but no compromise! If a region's to be thrown to the crocodiles, it won't be Unthank; upon that I am resolved. Monboddo is afraid of me: understandably. The hell with the standings, the top rung is up for grabs! All bets are off, the odds are cancelled, it's anybody's ballgame! The horses are all drugged, the track is glass . . . what is happening to my vocabulary?

(Gray 1981: 506)

As we have seen, the concern of many postmodern novels is precisely this: the simultaneity of power and subversion. While *Lanark* provides a critique of representation, it does so by virtually enacting the very power that is thematized and criticized in the novel.

In the section of *Postmodernist Fiction* entitled "Which reel?" Brian McHale notes that, in postmodern texts, movies and television appear as an ontological level: "a world-within-the world, often one in competition with the primary diegetic world of the text, or a plane interposed between the level of verbal representation and the level of the 'real'" (1987: 128). In postmodern fiction, cinematic discourse provides the illusion of visual representation. We have seen in *Lanark* how manipulative literally visual images can be. In *Midnight's Children* and *Daniel Martin* the visual images are described in language, not represented pictorially, but the illusion of perception is a powerful one, and is a way of creating an appearance of continuity and coherence. John Ellis, writing about cinema and Realism in *Visible Fictions*, points out that the visual images in film encourage the viewer to accept the "reality" of what is being seen: "Habitually, in a fiction film, vision is equated with access to truth: those who can see know more of the truth. . . . The position of the ultimate vision in any fiction film is not that of any of the characters, but that of the spectator" (Ellis 1982: 84). Indeed, the gaze of the spectator provides the link between possibly disparate scenes. Keith Cohen comments that there is an enforced absence of contradiction in cinematic images: "When two shots, mutually illogical, unconnected or even contradictory are brought together in film, the automatic and relentless flow of images forces at least the appearance of sequence. There is no such thing as a non sequitur in the movies" (Cohen 1979: 81).

Novels which use cinematic images often use them as a reference to a "reality" wherein situations and characters are fixed and specific. Roland Barthes, in *Camera Lucida*, comments that a photograph says "only and for certain *what has been*" (1984: 85), even if the camera eye is partial, in both senses of the word. Writing, Barthes says, cannot authenticate itself in the same way as a visual image can, and that is both its misfortune and its "voluptuous pleasure" (ibid.: 85). When visual images are described in language, however, their concreteness and specificity are undermined. In *The Implied Reader*, Wolfgang Iser describes this in terms of the difference between a novel, and the movie of the novel. In the first of these there are numerous possibilities (as many as there are readers) in terms, for example, of how a character is imagined to look or to sound. In the movie, however, these possibilities are narrowed down to "one complete and immutable picture" (Iser 1974: 283).

A "complete and immutable picture," though, is exactly what Saleem Sinai tries to create in *Midnight's Children* and, as we have seen in Chapter two, one of his techniques for creating a "whole" world is to use film vocabulary. In this way, he seeks to provide a sense of continuity of both content and form, so that the disparate events in his life appear to have a sequence. Indeed, plagued by decontextualized repetitions which threaten to de-form his narrative from the very beginning, Saleem urges his reader to "Watch" (Rushdie 1981: 12), as though this will help to give his narrative coherence. As he complains later in the novel: "The different parts of my somewhat complicated life refuse, with a wholly unreasonable obstinacy, to stay neatly in their separate compartments" (ibid.: 187). Since film is a representational medium, Saleem also makes reference to it in order to create both immediacy and the illusion of mimesis. Directions for the camera such as "close-up," "long-shot," and "fade-out," are short cuts which Saleem uses to try to efface novelistic techniques in favor of filmic ones. Relying on the reader to recognize what these phrases mean, Saleem is also relying on her/him to visualize the process. The cliché that "seeing is believing" is one which appears to inform Saleem's narrative, and through the cinematic techniques mentioned above, he tries to evoke the "truth" and continuity of his story. Thus, these same phrases help to create the "reality" of Bombay, the center of the Indian film industry, no native of which "should be without a basic film vocabulary" (Rushdie 1981: 109).

A recent advertizement for a Timeline World History Chart (1987) has the following caption: "The History Of The World Comes Alive When You See The Big Picture" (*The Atlantic*, Sept. 1987, 37). Visualizing here, has an almost magical quality, indeed a glance can resurrect 6,000 years of history. In the advertizement, a swirl of pictures emanates from the chart including a spaceship, Stonehenge, Christopher Columbus, and, oddly in this context, the Trojan Horse. The implication is that actually *seeing* the sequences of, and relationships between, historical events gives them a "reality" and an authority that merely *reading* about them apparently doesn't have. Saleem tries to create his own authority as a narrator through a similar process, by verbally creating a "big picture," in this case a cinema screen, on which to project his tale. Despite the erratic drift of memory, after all, he insists that it creates a "usually coherent version of events; and no sane human being ever trusts someone else's version more than his own" (Rushdie 1981: 211). Like a true Bombayite, Saleem is the camera through whose "eyes" we "see" the story of his life. Even his "talisman," the "memory of a large white bedsheet with a roughly circular hole some seven inches in diameter cut into the centre" (ibid.: 10), is a metaphoric camera and screen all in one. As did his grandfather Aadam, Saleem sees fragments through the omnipresent hole in the sheet, but the cinematic imagery gives the illusion that behind the sheet there is something waiting to be seen whole.

If Saleem's tale is subject to the authority of what is "seen," it is also at the mercy of the techniques and modes of the Bombay film industry, among the most prevalent of which is "melodrama." Interestingly, using melodramatic and clichéd techniques, which Saleem highlights by apologizing for them, is another way of creating the illusion of representation. Since his life is a mirror of India's, it is appropriate that it should occasionally acquire the "colouring of a Bombay talkie" (Rushdie 1981: 148). When Saleem is hit on the head by a flying spittoon, and his memory is wiped clean, the narrating Saleem writes:

> With some embarrassment, I am forced to admit that amnesia is the kind of gimmick regularly used by our lurid film-makers. Bowing my head slightly, I accept that my life has taken on, yet again, the tone of a Bombay talkie; but after all, leaving to one side the vexed issue of reincarnation, there is only a finite number of methods of achieving rebirth. So, apologizing for the melodrama. . . .
>
> (Rushdie 1981: 350)

Trying to comfort Padma, who responds with tears to the fate of the Sinai family, Saleem resorts to "movie Trailers," cheering her with promises of "next-attractions and coming-soons galore" (ibid.: 346). It is a clever technique to use, of course, because Padma cannot read, and, moving to the next part of his story, six years later, he fills in the gap with yet another visual cliché: "I permit myself to insert a Bombay-talkie-style close-up – a calendar ruffled by a breeze, its pages flying off in succession to denote the passing of the years; I superimpose turbulent long-shots of street riots, medium shots of burning buses and blazing English-language libraries . . ." (Rushdie 1981: 346).

Although Saleem uses cinematic vocabulary to give the illusion of an unmediated "reality," the images he employs are, none the less, written. We have already seen in Chapter two that the novel constantly reminds us of its textuality. Saleem's apparent authority is repeatedly undermined, both by his fragmented subjectivity and by his awareness of narrating and of being a narrative construct. While the film imagery gives the appearance of wholeness, this too is subverted by Saleem's narrative comments about the imagery he uses. It is interesting and significant that the two films that are described in the novel are both incomplete. Hanif's script about the ordinary life of a pickle factory which tries to incorporate all the possible conventions of Realism, is as much a fragment of "reality" as Saleem's text which it so closely resembles. It is never filmed, because it doesn't contain the elements of entertainment which would make it a viable, economically successful, project. Hanif's film, *The Lovers of Kashmir*, is interrupted by the announcement of

Mahatma Gandhi's death. Film's representational qualities are further undermined by Saleem's comment that

> Reality is a question of perspective; the further you get from the past, the more concrete and plausible it seems – but as you approach the present, it inevitably seems more and more incredible. Suppose yourself in a large cinema, sitting at first in the back row, and gradually moving up, row by row, until your nose is almost pressed against the screen. Gradually the stars' faces dissolve into dancing grain; tiny details assume grotesque proportions; the illusion dissolves – or rather, it becomes clear that the illusion itself *is* reality. . . .
>
> (Rushdie 1981: 165–6)

This comment shows an awareness of the illusion of representation in film. What is perceived as whole from a distance is gradually revealed to be the result of flickering projections of light. A film image, then, is composed of fragments and is neither a reflection of a whole world, nor an unmediated presentation of "reality."

A good example of the tension between mimesis and mediated perception is the fragment we "see" of *The Lovers of Kashmir*, which is later played out in "life" by Lal Quasim and Amina Sinai. The film is remarkable for its innovative subversion of the censor's regulations, which shows a consciousness of the process of creating a movie. As Saleem relies on his reader to visualize his cinematic phrases, so does Hanif rely on his viewers' knowledge of the conventions of censorship. Because actors and actresses were not allowed to touch one another on screen, Hanif's film has the lovers kissing, not one another, but things: "Pia kissed an apple, sensuously, with all the rich fullness of her painted lips; then passed it to Nayyar; who planted upon its opposite face, a virilely passionate mouth" (Rushdie 1981: 142). A similar scene occurs between Quasim and Amina which Saleem watches through the "dirty glass cinema-screen" (ibid.: 217) of the Pioneer Café. While "life," here, imitates "bad art" (ibid.: 217), it nevertheless does so through the mediation of Saleem's gaze. Seeing the scene between his mother and her first husband through the framed window, Saleem constructs it as a film, attributing to it all the self-consciousness and form of *The Lovers of Kashmir*: "What I'm watching here. . . is, after all, an

Indian movie" (Rushdie 1981: 217). The "film," however, is only representational because Saleem sees it that way, even in his re-creation of the incompleteness of the *Lovers*: "I left the movie before the end . . . wishing I hadn't gone to see it, unable to resist watching it all over again" (ibid.: 217).

The tensions and contradictions in the reader's position of reading cinematic references are most aptly described near the end of the novel when Saleem and the last of his long line of fathers, appropriately called Picture Singh, return to Bombay. Singh, a snake-charmer, engages in a competition to secure his title, "The Most Charming Man in the World." The show takes place in the Midnite-Confidential Club, an inky-black night-club where patrons can drink and romance cocooned in the "isolating, artificial night" (Rushdie 1981: 453). Like a cinema, the club is "for *now*, for nothing except right now" (ibid.: 454). Also, resembling cinematic light projection, the club has a spotlight, one which roves like a "luminary Russian roulette" (ibid.: 455), to make the patrons the subjects of the light's "voyeurism" (ibid.: 455). The waitresses, in keeping with the popular secrecy of the club, are blind, and on their closed eyelids are painted "unearthly luminous eyes" (ibid.: 453–4), parodying sight. In these "glowing eyes of blind women" (ibid.: 454), is a *mise en abyme* of Saleem's play with cinematic images. While he uses them to make the reader "see" a coherent whole, such sight is an artificial illusion.

Daniel Martin, in John Fowles' novel, *Daniel Martin*, tries to create a similar "big picture" to the one Saleem attempts in *Midnight's Children*. Indeed, he begins his novel with the authoritative statement: "Whole sight; or all the rest is desola-tion" (Fowles 1977a: 7). Daniel is a film script-writer who wishes to turn novelist, but is none the less limited by the demands of his own *métier*. This is, perhaps, why *Daniel Martin*, the novel he wishes to write but which can ultimately "never be read" (Fowles 1977a: 704), is in the style of a commercial cinema script of precisely the kind Daniel wishes to escape.

Daniel's reason for wanting to step off the screen is his dislike of his cinematic world persona. In "Games," the second chapter of the novel, he expresses his dismay at the artificiality of the Hollywood film world, and the eternal present tense in which it forces him to live. A call from his ex-sister-in-law Jane, telling him that her husband Anthony is dying and requesting his presence, gives Daniel an excuse to return to England and come to terms with his past. This self-discovery, he feels, will provide the opportunity to embark on a new, novelistic, career and a new, novelistic, persona. His life story, as film, would "betray the real thing" (Fowles, 1977a: 20), but the novel, which provides a "greater capacity for retreat" (ibid.: 308), would, he thinks, be a more appropriately mimetic genre:

> The film cannot be the medium of a culture all of whose surface appearances mislead, and which has made such a psychological art of escaping present, or camera, reality. For us English the camera, or public eye, invites performance, lying. We make abundant use of these appearances in our comedy, in our humour; socially and politically; but for our private reality we go elsewhere, and above all to words. Since we are so careful only to reveal our true selves in private, the "private" form of the read text must serve us better than the publicity of the seen spectacle.

> (Fowles 1977a: 306–7)

For Daniel, the novel is the best way to reveal his "true" self since, for him, it is a Realist medium. Film, on the other hand, usurps the individual imagination. Along with television it affects "all spheres of life where a free and independent imagination matters" (Fowles 1977a: 307). Both media "insidiously impose their own conformities, their angles, their limits of vision, deny the existence of what they cannot capture" (ibid.: 307). Daniel does, however, search for a way to inject Realism into his scripts, travelling to Egypt, for example, to help him focus on scenes he is writing about Kitchener in Egypt. It is interesting too, that his final moment of self-realization is prompted, not by a novel, but by the visual medium of a Rembrandt self-portrait in which he finds the epiphany he thought only existed in novel form: "the ultimate citadel of humanism" (Fowles 1977a: 703).

It goes without saying that Daniel is not a postmodern character, but an embodiment of Realist convention. However, *Daniel Martin* can be read as a critique, and even a send-up, of Daniel's rather moralistic sentiments. The cinematic language and techniques used throughout the novel make *Daniel Martin* the novel-of-the-(un-made) film rather than the more familiar film-of-the-novel. Cinematic and novelistic ploys are often at odds, as though Daniel's own war with both visual and linguistic images is being played out in the novel.

Unlike Saleem Sinai, Daniel Martin does not see film in representational terms. The "reality" it captures is one he finds illusory, and therefore he turns to the novel form as one which will imitate "the real structure of [his] racial being and mind" (Fowles 1977a: 371). He does, however, find the "objectivity of the camera" (ibid.: 72) appealing, and tries to incorporate this into his writing by favoring third over first-person narration: "how clear it was, if he ever did attempt the impossible [novel writing], that anything would be better than to present it in the first person" (ibid.: 73). Nevertheless, Daniel uses *both* first- and third-person narratives. In the Realist sense (which is the one Daniel favors) this split narration is a method of coming to terms with the "two people" (Fowles 1977a: 64) he insists he is. In cinematic terms, it is an attempt at narrative "suture," at joining together the "shored fragments" of his ruined self (ibid.: 19) into "one complete and immutable picture." As Kaja Silverman explains, an aspect of cinematic suture is the shot/reverse shot in which "the second shot shows the field from which the first shot is assumed to have been taken" (Silverman 1983: 201). The effect of this is to give the illusion of "whole sight," of the full 360° of a scene rather than the 180° of the camera eye. This technique effaces the presence of the camera since the camera always occupies the opposite field to the one the viewer sees. It is a method which *appears* to diminish the space between viewer and shot, and to give the illusion of an unmediated scene.

Daniel similarly tries to efface the subjectivity of the narrative "I" in favor of the apparent objectivity of the third-person. For this reason he rejects "S. Wolfe," the "hypothetical fictional projection of himself" (Fowles 1977a: 449) which has been suggested to him as a device for facilitating his novelistic auto-surgery. Since, as Barry Olshen points out, "S. Wolfe" is also an anagram of "Fowles" (Olshen 1978: 162), Daniel's rejection of him is a way of convincing the reader that *Daniel Martin* is unsullied by authorial intervention and is thus Daniel's true, unmediated history. Another device for creating the illusion of "reality" is through the "external" narratives included in the text. Jenny, Daniel's lover, and an actress playing a role in a movie for which Daniel has written the script, contributes to this seeming objectivity in the three chapters of the novel she writes. Although they are written as letters to Daniel, and occasionally address him as "you," they are primarily third-person, giving the appearance of honesty and objectivity. Since they include comments about events that Daniel also mentions, Jenny's chapters contribute to the illusion of "whole sight" into Daniel. They are thus examples of the cinematic shot/reverse shot technique since they allow the reader to both "see" Daniel and "see" how Daniel is being seen.

Because the shot/reverse shot "conceals the apparatus of enunciation" (Silverman 1983: 215), it has the illusory authority of "truth." "Truth" and "reality" are two of Daniel's main concerns, and although it is film, he feels, which fails to capture them, he is none the less unable to escape the traditional, cultural authority of the visual. In wanting to write his novel, Daniel wants to create a structure which will "tally better with the real structure" of his life: "something dense, interweaving, treating time as horizontal, like a skyline; not cramped, linear and progressive" (Fowles 1977a: 371). Yet, while the form of the novel is one composed of interwoven flashbacks and flashfor-wards, the cinematic imagery provides the illusion of linear continuity. Like Saleem Sinai, Daniel uses phrases such as "cut" (Fowles 1977a: 142), "close up" (ibid.: 172), and "one last shot" (ibid.: 425), and his insistence on seeing scenes "as if he were a camera, merely recording, at a remove from present reality" (ibid.: 597) subverts his desire for novelistic complexity. Visiting his ex-wife and her husband in a baronial manor, he sees the seating arrangement as approximating a film set: "We had gone into the drawing-room and sat around the fire in a loose circle, but that still left three-quarters of the room unoccupied. It was a little like a film set, one half expected a side open for the camera" (Fowles 1977a: 332). Similarly, when he meets Jane after many years, Daniel sees their discomfort with one another in cinematic terms: "For once the camera would have done better; the queries in eyes, the avoided looks, the hidden reservations on both sides, the self-consciousness" (ibid.: 176).

The artificiality of film is something Daniel despises. Ironically, however, using cinematic imagery in his novel highlights the artifice of both forms. This is noticeable in conversations between characters as well as in the "stock" situations Daniel reconstructs. In "The Harvest," the first chapter of the novel, and the most novelistic one, drawing as it does on similar scenes from Hardy's *Tess of the D'Urbervilles* and Lawrence's *The White Peacock*, quotation marks are eliminated as if to stress the visual quality of the scene. Although it is a moment from Daniel's past, it is written in a cinematic present tense. Here, the young Daniel, participating in the harvest ritual, is initiated into the cycle and the mysteries of life and death. The setting contrasts sharply with the scene of the second chapter, "Games," but is as much a construction as is Jenny's Hollywood apartment with its "fake Biedermeier table" (Fowles 1977a: 17). Like "The Harvest," "Games" is written in the present tense: "She stands and wanders across to the window, stubs out her cigarette – yes, she is acting – in a pottery dish by the telephone; then stares out, as he had, at the infamous city's artificial night" (Fowles 1977a: 18). Conversations, here, eschew the novelistic "she/he said" in favor of dialogue which, because written, can be difficult to follow:

"Proves my point."
"Well someone's fishing."
"Not even the smallest hook."
"You don't even . . . and you know it."
"Only by local standards."
"Balls."
"Darling, when you're – ."
"Oh Gawd, here we go again."
He is silent a moment. "When I was your age I could only look forward. At mine you . . ."
"Then you need your eyesight tested."

(Fowles 1977a: 19)

Clearly, this is an exchange which must be "seen to be believed." Like so much of the dialogue in *Daniel Martin*, it employs what Daniel's ex-wife calls "his B-movie sarcasms" (ibid.: 164), and clichés. As does the "melodrama" in *Midnight's Children*, the B-movie techniques in *Daniel Martin* create an illusion of representation, in this case, one of the "bourgeois melodrama" (ibid.: 643) of a Hollywood script.

Although he tries to conceal the apparatus of enunciation in his text (through the shot/reverse shot and the rejection of S. Wolfe) and despite his protestations about the camera's inability to represent his life, Daniel has a mania for being seen. Far from hiding in the "sacred combe" (Fowles 1977a: 306) of the novel, Daniel exhibits himself to the gaze of others, becoming "real" only when watched. Indeed, he occasionally makes a spectacle of himself in order to ensure that he *is* watched. At the coroner's inquest which follows Anthony's suicide, Daniel gives himself a pivotal role in confessing his sins. He makes the court into a set, the apparatus of which is focused on him: "I was not only legally but morally the guilty party in the divorce action. The real cause of war was a play I based on the circumstances of the divorce, but which travestied the true parts played in it by all concerned" (Fowles 1977a: 319).

It is noticeable that Daniel is drawn to women who watch him, and through whose (camera) eyes he is created. As a young boy, he has disdain for a girl who is "cross-eyed and wears spectacles" (Fowles 1977a: 101), but is attracted to Nancy Reed whose "summer-blue eyes do not squint. They stare at you . . . and make you hold your breath" (ibid.: 101). The consummation of his relationship with Jane, when both are Oxford students, is preceded by her "penetrating brown eyes, searching his . . . looking at him for the first time" (Fowles 1977a: 70). When he meets Jane again, many years later, he is attracted to her because of her angle of vision: " 'making him think' was essentially a making him look at himself through her eyes" (ibid.: 464). Similarly, Daniel's own looking at himself highlights the irreconcilable split between first- and third-person narration. As an Oxford student, he is dubbed "Mr. Specula Speculans" because his room has "at least fifteen mirrors" (Fowles 1977a: 61) on its walls. He dubs himself "Isherwood's camera, not unhappily reduced to watching himself, as if he were indeed a fiction, a paper person in someone else's script" (ibid.: 72).

Daniel is very much at the mercy of his *métier* and of the illusion of representation it affords. Interestingly, his looking at himself, becoming his own camera, as it were, makes the separation between his two selves clear. Daniel is not two people waiting to be joined into a whole, but a split subject, watching and watched. This is also the difference between intention and execution which further foregrounds his separate selves. Daniel *intends* to write a mimetic novel, but the self-consciousness of the novel form subverts this. He *intends* to get away from the "totalitarian" (Fowles 1977a: 308) regime of the commercial cinema, but finds himself subjected to its tyranny in a way which further undercuts "reality."

Caught between novel and cinema, *Daniel Martin* is a liminal text. This is signalled by the epigraph from Antonio Gramsci's *Prison Notebooks*: "The crisis consists precisely in the fact that the old is dying and the new cannot be born; in this interregnum a great variety of morbid symptoms appears" (Fowles 1977a: 3). Neither novel nor filmscript, *Daniel Martin* partakes of elements of both and in so doing highlights the "constructedness" of each. Although Daniel rejects the film world and its images, he is nevertheless bound by them. Similarly, while he consciously mentions that he is writing the novel ("the tiny first seed of what this book is trying to be . . ." (Fowles 1977a: 371); "it hasn't really distressed me till now when I set it down" (ibid.: 427)), he also denies it ("I couldn't write a novel about a scriptwriter. That would be absurd. A novelist who wasn't a scriptwriter might do it. But I'm a scriptwriter who isn't a novelist" (ibid.: 437). The final sentence of *Daniel Martin*, while it points back to the beginning of the novel, also points to re-reading of it as not-a-novel: "She laughed at such flagrant Irishry; which is perhaps why, in the end, and in the knowledge that Dan's novel can never be read, lies eternally in the future, his ill-concealed ghost has made that impossible last his own impossible first" (Fowles 1977a: 704). If Daniel's novel can never be read, it is because his intentions have been consistently subverted, both in his desire for mimesis and for whole sight which can be achieved by *neither* novel nor film.

In all three novels examined here, the allusion to visual images is an attempt to create a similar authority and Realism in prose as is apparently created in film and other specifically visual media. Products of a television-oriented culture, readers/viewers have been conditioned to the notion that something is real only if it is seen. Ironically, describing cinematic and other visual images in prose makes the artifice of the visual images abundantly clear. Phrases such as "cut," "long shot," and "close-up" are, after all, the language of film direction, and no one knows the "constructedness" of a film better than a director. This points to the process of creation rather than the finished, apparently unmediated, product. The cinematic images, *because* they are described in prose, have their authority undercut, and their "constructedness" highlighted.

As we have seen in *Daniel Martin* and *Midnight's Children*, the commercial, popular cinema is referred to as a short cut to Realist techniques and conventions. Popular cinema means continuity, closure, and an illusion of three-dimensionality which seems to present on screen a reflection of life as it "really" is. In fact, if Realism exists today at all, it does so most visibly in the media of the popular novel and film as well as in advertizing, television shows, and music videos. However, all of these use techniques similar to those found in the postmodern novel. Their aim, though, is not to question Realism but to mask it through the use of apparently subversive strategies. The following chapter, therefore, will examine some of the populist forms of Realism in the light of the challenge of postmodernism.

Appendix   Past the end of *Lanark*

Chapter 45

Paragraph 3:   "'Dont knife the leaf' is from the song *Lettuce Bleeds*" (Gray 1981: 488).

Paragraph 5:   "Grant's 'form of self-expression second only to the sneeze' is an Implag from Book 11 of the *Institutio Oratoria*" (ibid. 496).

Paragraphs 6, 7, 8: The battle between the cloth and wire monkeys (ibid.: 490).

Paragraph 9:   "The fine colours are taken from the anthology *Its Colours They are Fine*" (ibid. 497).

Chapter 46

Paragraph 1:   "'The sliding architecture of the waves' is from *Rudiment of an Eye*" (Gray 1981: 497).
"The peace-force led by Sergeant Alexander is blocked by God in a land whose shapes and colours come from *Ascent*" (ibid.: 496).

Chapter 47

"God's conduct and apology for it is an extended Difplag of the short story *Acid*" (Gray 1981: 491).

Paragraph 22: "Major Alexander's remark that 'Inadequate maps are better than no maps; at least they show that the land exists' is stolen from *The Kind of Poetry I Want* (ibid.: 493).

Chapter 48

Paragraph 2: "The Martian Headmaster is from the short story *Feathered Choristers*" (Gray 1981: 493).

Paragraph 8: "The batsman's wife is singing her own version of the song in the review *Something may come of it* (ibid.: 497).

Paragraph 15: "The android's method of cleaning the bed is a Difplag of *Jill the Gripper* from *Licking the Bed Clean*" (ibid.: 496).

Paragraph 22: "The cursive adder is from the poem *Movements*" (ibid.: 493).

"The android's circuitous seduction of God is from the play, *The Android Circuit*" (ibid.: 493).

Paragraph 25: "The android's discovery by the Goddess is a Difplag of *The Hickie*" (ibid.: 492).

Chapter 49

"General Alexander's requiem for Rima is a Blockplag of *Placenta*" (Gray 1981: 492).

Paragraph 49: " 'Down the crater of Vesuvius in a tramcar' is a remark attributed to General Douglas Haig in *Quips from the Trenches*" (ibid.: 498).

All of the above constitute a "mock-military excursion" which is "an extended Difplag of Xenophon's *Anabasis*" (ibid.: 498).

Chapter 50

" 'In a wee while, dearie' is an Implag of the poem 'The Voyeur'" (Gray 1981: 492).

Index ends "in Hyper-Utopian Euphoria" (ibid.: 498–9).

Conclusion: Stephen King
and Beyond

In a society where life tends to imitate television, the start of a new fall season provides a revealing portrait of current American obsessions, fears, myths and trends.

Heather Robinson 1987: 69

Realism, in the sense that it has been discussed in this study, is a prevalent force in popular culture. Television shows and advertizements, commercial cinema and popular fiction are, ironically, inheritors and perpetrators of Realist dogma. This is particularly ironic in historical terms because Realism came to be, as exemplified by the writings of Matthew Arnold and F. R. Leavis, a defense against popular culture in favor of "high" cultural values. In his educational programe, *Culture and Environment*, Leavis argued against popular entertainment and advertizements, and for a system of education which would inform the "taste and sensibility" (Leavis and Thompson 1964: 1) of the élite. Indeed, in *For Continuity* he asks: "can a hundred D. H. Lawrences preserve even the idea of emotional sincerity against the unremitting, pervasive, masturbatory manipulations of 'Scientific' Publicity, and what is the same thing, commercially supplied popular art?" (1933: 105). The effect of this separation of "high" and "low" cultures has been the canonization, not only of certain texts, but also of attitudes which reproduce the split. In "Postmodernism and Consumer Society," Frederic Jameson points out that postmodernism has questioned these boundaries and separations,

> most notably the erosion of the older distinction between high culture and so-called mass culture. This is perhaps the most

distressing development of all from an academic standpoint, which has traditionally had a vested interest in preserving the realm of high or elite culture against the surrounding environment of philistinism, of schlock and kitsch, of T.V. series and *Reader's Digest* culture. . . .

(Jameson 1985: 112)

There are, indeed, structural similarities, if ideological differences, between the postmodern novels discussed in previous chapters and some of the manifestations of popular culture. As I will argue in my discussion of Stephen King's *Misery*, however, metafictional techniques are used in popular culture to give an *illusion* of audience co-creation. The playfulness and novelty of these techniques are used, not to foster critique and subversion, but to sell products. Thus they mask, rather than reveal, the dominant ideology behind them.

Television and advertizing[1] share with the Realists a sense of absolute value and an impetus toward didacticism. Consider, for example, the ideology proposed by most television emanations where a discrete and easily definable "good" triumphs over an equally recognizable "evil." The "evil" can range from assault to a lack of personal hygiene, and the "good" from a successful trial verdict to deodorant soap. (In "Westerns" this split is often signalled by the "good" cowboys' white hats and the "bad" cowboys' black ones. These are agreed-upon semiotic signposts which allow for the kind of parodies found in movies such as *Blazing Saddles* or *The Draughtsman's Contract*.) No matter what the specifics, however, there is the assumption of "common sense" in this structure, of a shared notion of what constitutes (and semiotically signals) "good" and "evil," and of the desirability of one over the other. In television shows, even for the most part in serials, closure is produced by the reassurance of a criminal brought to justice or a domestic misunderstanding resolved. Advertizing uses the same structure to present a problem, a rupture in the social "norm" which, it assures its audience, is common to all. Halitosis, acne, perspiration odor, or stringy hair are all apparently rampant, but can be solved by a timely application of the advertized product. The viewing subject, then, is him- or herself formed into an acceptable product, a "whole," it is implied, free from the social indiscretions caused by the above problems. The viewer is encouraged to "identify" with seemingly "real life" characters and situations whose own difficulties are solved by the purchase of the advertisers' "goods." In this way, they participate in what Jeffrey Schrank calls a "feedback loop." Ads "reflect a society they have helped to educate, and part of the advertising reflection is the effect of advertising itself" (Schrank 1977: 104). Marriages, jobs, friendships, and whole corporations can be saved, it would seem, by garbage bags, bathroom cleaners, or detergents which eliminate the embarrassment of ring-around-the-collar. There is a sense of truth, absolute value, and coherence produced by these ads, and indeed by most television programming which, it would be argued, is similar to the ideology proposed by the Realists.

If television is, as McLuhan suggests (1960: xi), a global village, then it is a place where an illusion of coherent, individual subjects rules. The illusion is created that the individual has power and control over the choices that he or she makes, rather than being controlled by, and subjected to, the ideology which in fact has the ultimate authority. Thus television creates the choices which lead to an illusion of individual freedom. As Schrank points out, this is "pseudo-choice," and it masks its own conditions of production:

> In pseudo-choice, the world is a multiple-choice test. We are free to answer questions only in terms of the options presented. A real-choice test would have only blank spaces for our answers which would be unshaped by the test maker. A multiple-choice test offers real choices but only the illusion of freedom.
>
> (Schrank 1971: 12)

Part of the power of the pseudo-choice offered by advertizing is in its apparent gift of knowledge which will make the viewers into seemingly more acceptable social beings. Viewers "know," for example, that the cure for a cold is "Contac-C" and that the answer to bad breath is "Listerine." The illusion of individual power is also created by less obvious ideological manipulation. For example, in his lecture "Bus Plunges and Weather Forecasting: Reassurance in the Age of Reagan," Alexander Cockburn (1987) comments on the implications of the twenty-four hour, nationwide weather broadcasts on an American pay-television channel. According to Cockburn, viewers are transfixed by this "non-information." One of its effects is to downplay the disorienting problems of politics and economics, and to give the viewer a sense of control because he or she knows, in Vermont, that it is raining in California. It also promotes a sense of coherence, fostering the illusion that we are all in this weather together.

The metafictional techniques used in various aspects of popular culture tend to work toward maintaining this illusion. In *Reading Television*, John Fiske and John Hartley comment that television is, to some extent, becoming self-critical:

> A large amount of television comedy directs quite telling parodies at television itself. Programmes celebrating broadcasting anniversaries often show archive material that of itself helps to demystify the medium by giving present-day viewers a point of comparison. Several programmes have resurrected sequences of previously edited-out material showing disasters and mistakes occurring during the production of otherwise serious programmes.
>
> (Fiske and Hartley 1978: 194)

However, this self-consciousness has not yet reached the point where it changes or questions the control or the ideology behind television. Indeed, the authority of Realism is maintained in popular culture at the expense of a relativism which might topple financial empires. Ronald Sukenick addresses this issue in *In Form: Digressions on the Art of Fiction*. In arguing against Gerald Graff's idea that challenges to authority are dangerous because we need authority to combat dogmatic systems of thought, and that relativism paves the road to mass social manipulation, he writes:

> But very much of what Graff says is reversible. Is it a critical relativism that smooths the path to totalitarianism, or is it, in our society, acceptance of political dogma and consumerist cliché? Is it radical esthetics that encourages a mindless consumer society, or is it that conventional mimetic realism which provides the basis for all those blockbusters in the box office and on the best seller list? . . . Is it not all the more urgent, given the pressures of that [consumerist] manipulation,

to present the reader with a literature that gives him models for a creative truth of "construction" rather than a passive truth of "correspondence," for confrontation and recreation rather than a reconciliation and adjustment through the identification and catharsis inherent in mimetic theory . . .?

(Sukenick 1985: 236)

The appearance of relativism in popular culture, however, tends, paradoxically, to reinforce precisely what it undermines in postmodern fiction, and it does so by making the "passive truth of correspondence" less overt. For example, the British and Canadian Benson and Hedges cigarette ads use strategies of displacement, in which the cigarette package becomes, for example, an electric plug, a fish, a treasure chest or a parrot. Like postmodern novels, these ads draw attention to their processes, and often involve the viewer to the extent that he or she has to search for the package as if in a puzzle. In one ad., the letters have been blown from the package by a fan, and the viewer has to reconstruct them. Judith Williamson comments that, while these advertisements do what all ads do – "re-place a product in a context in which it has no 'natural' connection, so that it takes on meaning from its surroundings" – the difference is that "the B&H ads don't seek to naturalize this re-location, they play on its strangeness" (1985: 69). However, as Williamson also points out, this strangeness implies ideological assumptions about class, taste, and Art: "The ads are visual puzzles, they imply meanings one doesn't have access to. This suggests 'High Art' and thereby, exclusivity. A product for the discerning, the tasteful, the few" (Williamson 1985: 69). Like most ads, these ones work by a process of "identification," in Sukenick's terms. The viewer who can solve the puzzle is hailed by the ad. (in the Althusserian sense), and is thus created as a subject.

This is also the case in music videos. These are, after all, advertizements for records, and the sales tactic is to make the viewer identify with the members of the band who perform in the video. They work in similarly clever ways to those used in the B&H ads. Some play with the act of reading and intertextual reference, parodying, for example, techniques used in Flaubert's *Madame Bovary* or Cervantes' *Don Quixote*. Larry Gowan's *A Criminal Mind*, Ultravox's *Love's Great Adventure*, and Aha's

Take On Me all deal with levels of fiction and "reality" as characters are pulled into the adventure stories or comic books they are reading. These levels are drawn to the reader's attention through graphics which simulate cartoons or line drawings in a book. In the Ultravox video, the character is so out of breath from his heroic adventures that he has to request that the camera and the music pause while he regains his composure. These videos create their audiences by offering a spirit of adventure. It is clear in this latter video, for example, that the survival techniques learned by the characters through their reading are applicable, too, to "life." When "thugs" attack the reading lead singer, he is able to overcome them because of the "adventure" he has had through reading.

Other videos call attention to their apparatuses of enunciation which seem to subvert the mimesis of the story. A narrative video by Genesis called *Illegal Alien*, for example, follows three Mexicans' attempts to gain legal status in the United States. Having been through the forms and the photographs, the characters gather together. They gaze expectantly upwards in a parody of new arrivals to Ellis Island. As the camera pulls back, however, it reveals not the Statue of Liberty, but a catwalk, more cameras, and the flats of the set. The expectant gazes, therefore, are toward the true process of alien-(n)ation. However, this video works in much the same way as the twenty-four hour weather channel. The situation, here, is conveyed largely through clichéd images. The Mexicans wear dark glasses, and they look seedy and uncomfortable in their suits. They pay money to a shifty character who can get them a deal on immigration papers. This enforces a sense of ideological coherence (among American viewers). It allows "us" to recognize "ourselves" through the differences from shady, undesirable "them."

While similar admissions of contrivance and parody are found in some television shows, their purpose is not demystification. Since television shows function by attracting advertizing, they have to maintain an ideological agenda commensurate with what the advertisers wish to promote. In *Moonlighting*, a show which overtly plays with metafictional techniques, scenes from *Casablanca*, *The Taming of the Shrew*, *The Honeymooners*, and *Blazing Saddles* are represented. In one episode, the criminal runs through a studio set, hotly pursued by detectives. Seeing a "cowboy" dressed in black, seated on a black horse, the criminal asks him if he is a "bad guy." Assured that this is the case, the criminal identifies himself as a "bad guy" and asks for a lift. In other episodes, actors and actresses step out of character to create an illusion-within-the-illusion. They comment on fan mail, the talents of the writers, and the development of the plot. At one point, a character consults his watch and announces that, as there are only ten minutes remaining in the show, they had better catch the criminal quickly. Despite the inventiveness of these and other situations, however, there is a distinct lack of any political motivation behind them. Again, novelty is the driving force, even though closure is always asserted and a clear morality is maintained.

These latter also undermine the rather clever techniques of *Max Headroom*. This show is clearly about television. In the opening episode, Max is created when a reporter, Edison Carter, who is researching an advertizing crime ("blipverts," subliminal advertizing images which flash on the T.V. screens in such rapid succession they create information overload and explode viewers' brain cells), is chased into a parking garage by the advertizers. Here, he crashes into an overhead beam whose "Max Headroom" is too low. While he is lying unconscious, his co-workers try to match the electrical impulses in his brain to a computer circuit and Max is born. The program plays on the reporter's split subjectivity, since Max shares memories with him, although he soon develops a personality all his own. The cleverness of this show lies in its sometimes savage criticism of television. It is set in a future where the only thing people do is watch television. Advertizers and other manipulators, therefore, battle for control of the television medium, and the criticism of them is often quite striking. What undermines this otherwise hopeful show, is that the distance between the future in which it is set and "now" is clearly maintained. The criticism, therefore, is immediately watered down (not "us," but "them"). Another problem is that the "bad" advertizers are always overcome in the end by the "good" reporter, and all the possibilities are thus subverted by the very dominating force that is so explicitly criticized.

The seeming self-consciousness in television and advertizing is also apparent in popular fiction. However, as in the forms of popular culture, the techniques and playfulness of postmodernism are used without any of its strategies of subversion. To examine this in more detail, I have chosen Stephen King's novel, *Misery*, as an archetypal example of popular fiction. The techniques used here are similar to the ones I have discussed in relation to postmodern fiction, although the motivation behind them is quite different. I have chosen Stephen King because his movies and novels have made his name synonymous with popular culture, and *Misery*, because of both its play with metafiction and its popularity – it spent more than twenty weeks on *The New York Times'* best-seller list.

In *Misery*, Paul Sheldon, a writer of best-selling Gothic romance novels, wakes up after a car crash in which he has shattered his legs to find himself the patient and prisoner of a psychotic former nurse, Annie Wilkes. Annie is, as she repeatedly tells Paul, his "number-one fan" (King 1987: 6), but this does not prevent her from torturing him for what she sees as serious lapses in his behavior. These misdemeanors range from complaining to swearing to attempting escape (for which she cuts off his left foot with an axe). His most serious mistake, however, has been to kill off the much-loved heroine of his novels, Misery Chastain, so that he might quit the realm of popular fiction for a career as a "serious" writer. This becomes a life-threatening decision, particularly because Annie's devotion to the character has conditioned her reaction to Paul: " 'You're good,' she said gently, 'I *knew* you would be. Just reading your books, I knew you would be. A man who could think of Misery Chastain, first think of her and then *breathe life* into her, could be nothing else'" (King 1987: 18). When Annie discovers that Misery has died in childbirth, she is dangerously enraged but nevertheless decides to save Paul from the error of his ways. Using the codeine she gives him for the pain in his legs, and to which he has become addicted, Annie bribes Paul into burning the manuscript of *Fast Cars*, the only copy of a book he feels might have won him "*next year's American Book Award*" (King 1987: 14). *Fast Cars* is the story of "a slum kid trying to get out of a bad environment" (ibid.: 20), but its confusing plot, play with time and, above all, its profanity have convinced Annie that it has "no nobility" (ibid.: 20). Once it is safely burned, however, Paul is free to do penance: to resurrect what Annie feels is his true talent, and with it to bring Misery Chastain back to life. To this end, she buys him an old typewriter although, since in the course of his writing it spits out several letters (n, t, e), he, and Annie, have to fill in the blanks by hand.

Misery has all the elements of a best-selling chriller: suspense, claustrophobia, terror, unpredictability, and rats. However, it also uses techniques which are common to metafiction. The novel is, in a sense, about fiction writing and, in this case, life and art are intimately connected on the level of plot since Paul, like Scheherezade, must entertain his audience with stories in order to stay alive. Portions of *Misery's Return* are reproduced in the text in a different type-face from that used in the rest of the book, with the missing letters "handwritten" in ink. There are allusions to other texts and fictional characters, most obviously to Scheherezade (King 1987: 60ff.), the death and resurrection of Sherlock Holmes (ibid.: 230), and to John Fowles' *The Collector* (ibid.: 151, 209). Paul also comments, at some length, about writing, readers, and about the relationship of "serious" to popular fiction. On the level of plot, the novel examines the nature of power, although this is a common technique for producing the terror in horror fiction. Annie certainly has power over Paul by virtue of his infirmity and his dependence on codeine. She seems, however, to be overthrown: Paul does eventually gather the strength to fight back by setting what Annie thinks is the finished manuscript of *Misery's Return* on fire. In the ensuing struggle, she trips over the typewriter and fractures her skull.

However, Annie has a more tenacious power over Paul, and this is one that is only obliquely questioned by the novel. Annie is a Realist reader, yet part of the tension in the novel derives from the issue of whether it is she who exerts control over the writer, or whether her prediction for mimesis is produced by the ideology created in, for example, the Misery stories. While she recognizes that fiction has conventions, she is a reader who demands coherence, continuity, and, above all, fair play. Her reaction to Misery's death shows that she is, on some level, aware that the conventions of fiction are contrived:

In my job I saw dozens of people die – *hundreds*, now that I think about it. Sometimes they go screaming and sometimes they go in their sleep – they just slip away, the way you said, sure.

But characters in stories DO NOT just slip away! God takes us when he thinks it's time and a writer is God to the people in a story, he made them up just like God made US up and no one can get hold of God to make him explain, all right, okay, but as far as Misery goes I'll tell you one thing you dirty bird, I'll tell you that God just happens to have a couple of broken legs and God just happens to be in MY house eating MY food. . . and. . . .

(King 1987: 33)

However, it is clear that Annie judges fictional conventions only by the standards of her immediate experience. The profane language in *Fast Cars*, for example, is not "realistic" to her because she doesn't use it: "What do you think I do when I go to the feed store in town? What do you think I *say*? 'Now Tony, give me a bag of that effing pig feed and a bag of that bitchly cow-corn and some of that Christing ear-mite medicine'. . . . 'You didn't have to use such words in the Misery books, because they didn't use such words at all back then'" (King 1987: 20, 21). She also gets angry when Paul refuses to treat his writing as "natural" when he "pervert[s] the talent God gave [him] by calling it a business" (ibid.: 66). Finally, Annie is insistent that Paul's resurrection of Misery should be done fairly. Thus, when he begins *Misery's Return* with reference to a scene that didn't happen in the previous novel, Annie calls it a cheat (King 1987: 98), and demands a clearer, more "realistic" continuity.

To Paul, Annie is "the perfect audience, a woman who loved stories without having the slightest interest in the mechanics of making them. She was the embodiment of that Victorian archetype, Constant Reader. She did not want to hear about his concordances and indices because to her Misery and the characters surrounding her were perfectly real" (King 1987: 57). As "Constant Reader" Annie fits into a parade of readers (and viewers) whose involvement with art – "even of such a degenerate sort as popular fiction" (ibid.: 230) – is all-consuming. Considering, however, that Annie is a psychotic, paranoid murderer who has catatonic trances whenever Paul mentions the technical or business side of his craft, this is an oddly insulting portrait of the "Constant Reader." Considering, too, that Stephen King's novels are included in the realm of popular fiction and that they probably have many "Constant Readers," this would seem to undermine, indeed to forbid, any process of co-creation. This ideal reader is (as Annie is) blind to (and perhaps, as viewers are with television, encouraged to remain blind to) the process and techniques of popular culture. This is, perhaps, why the metafictional conventions used in the novel do not question, subvert, or in any way threaten the Realist ideology of *Misery* since, it is implied here, the "perfect audience" would have little interest in such radical participation.

There is always the possibility that King is using these techniques to attract a different reader from the one he so vigorously insults. Perhaps he is seeking to achieve a complicity between himself and a "serious" academic audience. However, his use of postmodern elements is not unlike that of advertizers who use "high art" forms in order to give viewers an illusion of sophistication. It is a tribute to the infinite resourcefulness of capitalism that these "high art" forms are co-opted by the market. "Classical" music and paintings are used in commercials for everything from tea to chocolate bars, and the implication is that viewers can be painlessly initiated into the apparent mysteries of the "greats." Viewers "know," for example, that the Mona Lisa's enigmatic smile is the result of her having consumed a Cadbury's Caramilk bar. Similarly, advertizers who use postmodern techniques do so to provide reassurance that viewers are on the cutting edge of an avant-garde which is uncomplicated and easily understood. Like these advertizers, King allows his readers the cachet of initiates into the avant-garde of postmodern techniques, but without the difficulty of having to struggle with the philosophy behind them. He creates an apparently sophisticated audience, however, in order to conceal that he is likening his readers to Annie Wilkes.

Annie is especially conscious of keeping up appearances. Having been tried for, and acquitted of, a series of murders (which she did, in fact, commit), she is aware that any scratch on the veneer she maintains might arouse her neighbors' malevolence. Thus, her land is carefully maintained and everything seems in perfect working order, despite the clearly damaged mind behind it. Although Annie is playing a role here, the difference between appearance and "reality" is not an example of split subjectivity. These two aspects of Annie are, in this novel, facets of what is presented as a unified, however unbalanced, self. The causes of her illness are not explored here; only the mask she uses to hide it is important. Just as Annie plays a role to keep up appearances, so does the novel use self-conscious techniques to mask an essentially Realist ideology. The moral tone of the novel begins in the acknowledgements where the (ab)use of such drugs as the ones Annie gives Paul is explained to the reader who may not be aware of their dangers: "There is, of course, no such drug as Novril, but there are several codeine-based drugs similar to it, and, unfortunately, hospital pharmacies and medical practice dispensaries are sometimes lax in keeping such drugs under tight lock and close inventory" (King 1987: v). The condescension to the "Constant Reader" is continued in the parody of reader-participation afforded by the typewriter's missing letters. Annie helps Paul fill in the letters, but this is as much co-creation as she is allowed; although, when he complains to her about the missing letters, Annie cuts off Paul's thumb with an electric carving knife, which actively hinders his creative process. It is also significant that the intertextual references in *Misery* are, for the most part, overtly signalled. Actual references are made to the most obvious ones mentioned above. Paul, for example, wonders whether Annie has "John Fowles' first novel on her shelves and decide[s] it might be better not to ask" (King 1987: 151). For a reader who might not know what John Fowles' first novel is, a quotation from *The Collector* provides the epigraph to Book Three (ibid.: 209).

There are, however, less overtly-stated references to other best-selling Fowles novels, which is interesting considering that Fowles, despite his sophisticated play with metafictional conventions, is a highly moralistic writer. As I discussed in Chapter three, Fowles is quite insulting to his readers in the preface to the revised edition of *The Magus*, not only in assuming that those who enjoy it have "adolescent" (Fowles 1977b: 9) sensibilities, but also in his elitist despair at letters which treat his novels as "crossword puzzles, with only one set of correct answers behind the clues . . . ('Dear Mr. Fowles, Please explain the significance of . . .')" (ibid.: 9). Paul, in *Misery*, similarly despairs of readers with what he calls "*the Scheherezade complex*" (King 1987: 231), in which they become so involved in the novelistic world that they seek to recreate it in their own. Thus, he tells of two letters from fans suggesting Misery theme parks (ibid.: 231), and another from a woman who had turned an upstairs room in her home into Misery's parlour, complete with authentic period furniture (ibid.: 232–3). Another intertextual reference is to "Poor Koko," a story in Fowles' collection *The Ebony Tower* (1974) in which a writer's manuscript, for a book on Thomas Love Peacock, is burned by a burglar who breaks into his cottage when he refuses to write a novel based on the life of the burglar. In exploiting both metafictional techniques and intertextual references, however, Stephen King's novel, like Fowles' novels, only thinly veils Realist ideology.

In John Fowles' *Daniel Martin*, Daniel ruefully justifies his continuing work in commercial cinema with the comment that "Audience corrupts. Even more than power" (Fowles 1977a: 190). In *Misery* Paul's immediate audience, Annie, is certainly described, along with the examples Paul gives of other "Constant Readers" (of Conan Doyle, Charles Dickens, and John Galsworthy (King 1987: 230–3)), as a corrupting influence. When Paul first sees Annie, he is reminded of the graven images of goddesses. She is like the stone idols "worshipped by superstitious African tribes in the novels of H. Rider Haggard" (King 1987: 7). As both "Constant Reader" and idol Annie becomes an allegorical figure, and the battle for control between Paul and Annie becomes an allegorical battle. On this level, her bribing Paul with drugs to burn his "serious" manuscript and create a "degenerate" one is a metaphor for the ideology of a popular culture which actively promotes the lack of critical engagement which might lead to the questioning, and even subversion, of that ideology. Annie, indeed, appears to win the battle between writer and reader. Even though Paul escapes to continue his "serious" work, the spirit of Annie still haunts him: "Annie Wilkes was in her grave. But, like Misery Chastain, she rested there uneasily. In his dreams and waking fantasies, he dug her up again and again. You couldn't kill the goddess. Temporarily drug her with bourbon, maybe, but that was all" (King 1987: 307). However, while the vicious "Constant Reader" appears to exert a mind-numbing control here, the ultimate power in *Misery* still rests with the author. (This jockeying for position by reader and writer is, interestingly, a ploy used by Fowles in *The French Lieutenant's Woman* (1969). While there are three endings to the novel, and the reader is theoretically free to close the book after whichever ending he or she chooses, the tyranny of both the author and the last chapter exerts the strongest control.) A reader whose concern is purely for stories, *Misery* implies, could not really be interested in contesting authority. The last lines of the novel, therefore, are neither Paul's nor Annie's but Stephen King's authoritative assertion of closure: "Lovell, Maine: September 23rd, 1984/Bangor, Maine: October 7th, 1986: *Now my tale is told*" (King 1987: 310). The phrase refers to that engraved on one of Annie's ceramic statues: a penguin standing on a block of ice which bears the caption. *Misery* is, indeed, published by Viking/*Penguin* and the final lines are a double assertion of both authorial control and of the status of the book as product. In the novel's undermining of its reader it is indeed maintaining a control which denies any questioning of its Realist conventions. It creates (as does television), a passive consumer of ideology. Realism persists, therefore, in reproducing the conditions of its production in today's popular culture by asserting the accuracy of its reflection of "life," and by contriving to diffuse the potentially polemical workings of its metafictional veneer. Realism has not disappeared, but it is being challenged – and *that* is the function of postmodern fiction today.

Notes

Preface

1 Marx and Engels used ideology to mean illusion or "false consciousness." It has also been used as a designation of a rigid system of belief (usually Marxist), which is not founded in experience. In the sense that I am using it throughout this study, ideology is a general system of beliefs held by a given group which are powerful because unexamined. These beliefs are unconscious because they create preconceptions usually assumed to be a reflection of the "way it is."

   For further information see Raymond Williams, *Keywords* (Glasgow: Collins, 1976: 126–30).

2 For the terms of the debate see: Brian McHale, *Postmodernist Fiction* (New York and London: Methuen, 1987); Douwe Fokkema and Hans Bertens (eds), *Approaching Postmodernism* (Amsterdam and Philadelphia: John Benjamins, 1986); Hal Foster (ed.), *Postmodern Culture* (London and Sydney: Pluto, 1983); Jean-François Lyotard, *The Postmodern Condition: A Report on Knowledge* (Minneapolis: University of Minnesota Press, 1984); Linda Hutcheon, *The Poetics of Postmodernism: History, Theory, Fiction* (New York and London: Routledge, 1988).

3 For discussions of the social and political reasons behind the rise of Realism see: Terry Eagleton, *Literary Theory* (Minneapolis: University of Minnesota Press, 1983); George J. Becker (ed.), *Documents of Modern Literary Realism* (Princeton: Princeton University Press, 1963); George J. Becker, *Realism in Modern Literature* (New York: Ungar, 1980); Damian Grant, *Realism* (London: Methuen, 1970); Patrick Parrinder, *Authors and Authority: A Study of English Literary Criticism and its relation to Culture* 1750–1900 (London: Routledge, 1977); Ian Watt, *The Rise of the Novel* (Harmondsworth: Penguin, 1957), F.W.J. Hemmings (ed.), *The Age of Realism* (Harmondsworth: Penguin, 1974).

Chapter one   Realism and its discontents

1 Realism as a scientific and philosophical term will not be dealt with here. For discussions see: George J. Becker, *Realism in Modern Literature* (New York: Ungar, 1980); Damian Grant, *Realism* (London: Methuen, 1970); Alice R. Kaminsky, "On Literary Realism," *The Theory of the Novel*, ed. John Halperin (London: Oxford University Press 1974); John Passmore, *A Hundred Years of Philosophy* (Harmondsworth: Penguin, 1968), especially 258–97.

2 For a discussion of this see: Erich Auerbach, *Mimesis*, trans. Willard R. Trask (Princeton: Princeton University Press, 1974).

3 For an in-depth study of the development of moral criticism see: Chris Baldick, *The Social Mission of English Criticism, 1848–1932* (Oxford: Oxford University Press, 1983).

4 For the first of these see: George Levine, "Realism Reconsidered," *The Theory of the Novel*, ed. John Halperin (London: Oxford University Press, 1974); Erich Heller, "The Realistic Fallacy," *Documents of Modern Literary Realism*, ed. George J. Becker (Princeton: Princeton University Press, 1963).

  For the second, see: Michael Bell, *The Sentiment of Reality* (London: Allen, 1983); J. P. Stern, *On Realism* (London: Routledge, 1973).

5 See, for example: W. B. Michaels and Stephen Knapp, "Against Theory," *Critical Inquiry* 8 (1982): 723–42; Gerald Graff, "The Myth of the Postmodernist Breakthrough," *Tri-Quarterly* 26 (1973): 383–417; Gerald Graff and Reginald Gibbons (eds), *Criticism in the University* (Evanston, Illinois: Northwestern University Press, 1985).

  The issue is examined in some detail in: Paul de Man, *The Resistance to Theory* (Minneapolis: University of Minnesota Press, 1986).

Chapter two   Telling li(v)es: History and historiographic metafiction

1 Barbara Foley makes this point in reference to what she calls the "metahistorical" novel: "Where the realistic historical novel introduced empirical data to corroborate its thematic statements, the metahistorical novel brings in historical documentation to highlight the provisional and indeterminate nature of historical knowledge" (*Telling the Truth*, 1980: 230).

2 I am using the term "social formation" in the sense that it is proposed in Belsey's *Critical Practice*: "Ideology . . . works in conjunction with political practice and economic practice to constitute the *social formation*, a formulation which promotes a more complex and radical analysis of social relations than the familiar term, 'society', which often evokes either a single homogeneous mass, or alternatively a loosely connected group of autonomous individuals, and thus offers no challenge to the assumptions of common sense" (1980: 5).

Chapter three Postmodern performance

1 See, for example, Michel Benamou and Charles Caramello (eds), *Performance in Postmodern Culture* (Madison, Wisconsin: Coda Press Inc., 1977).
2 There is no satisfactory English translation of this term, although "microcosm" probably comes closest. For discussion see Lucien Dällenback, *Le récit spéculaire* (Paris: Editions du Seuil, 1977), and Linda Hutcheon, "Thematizing Narrative Artifice: Parody, Allegory, and the *Mise En Abyme*" in *Narcissistic Narrative: The Metafictional Paradox* (New York and London: Methuen, 1984).

Chapter four Unmastering masterful images

1 Quoted on the dust jacket of the American edition of *Lanark*.

Conclusion: Stephen King and beyond

1 The dominant popular culture of my experience as a Canadian is, of course, American not British. The structure of the television shows and advertizements I am referring to, therefore, is limited to the American models.

Bibliography

Anon. (1970) Review of *Ivanhoe*, by Walter Scott, in John O. Hayden (ed.), *Scott: The Critical Heritage*, New York: Barnes and Noble: 188–94.

—— (1970) Review of *Quentin Durward*, by Walter Scott, in John O. Hayden (ed.), *Scott: The Critical Heritage*, New York: Barnes and Noble: 272–8.

Abrams, M. H. (1953) *The Mirror and the Lamp*, Oxford: Oxford University Press.

—— (1971) *A Glossary of Literary Terms*, 3rd ed., New York: Holt.

Ackroyd, Peter (1985) *Hawksmoor*, London: Hamish Hamilton.

Alter, Robert (1975) *Partial Magic*, Berkeley: University of California Press.

Althusser, Louis (1977) "Ideology and Ideological State Apparatuses," *Lenin and Philosophy and Other Essays*, trans. Ben Brewster, New York and London: Monthly Review Press: 127–86.

Aristotle (1967) *Poetics. Literary Criticism: Plato to Dryden*, trans. and ed. Allan H. Gilbert, Detroit: Wayne State University Press.

Arnold, Matthew (1909) *Essays in Criticism*, ed. S. R. Littlewood, London: Macmillan.

—— (1970) "The Function of Criticism at the Present Time," *Matthew Arnold: Selected Prose*, ed. P. J. Keating, Harmondsworth: Penguin: 130–56.

Auerbach, Erich (1946) *Mimesis: The Representation of Reality in Western Literature*, trans. Willard R. Trask, Princeton University Press, 1974.

Austen, Jane (1972) *Northanger Abbey*, ed. Anne Henry Ehrenpreis, Harmondsworth: Penguin.

Baldick, Chris (1985) "Estrangements," Review of *Metafiction*, by Patricia Waugh, *Times Literary Supplement*, 15 March: 295.

—— (1983) *The Social Mission of English Criticism*, Oxford: Oxford University Press.

Barnes, Julian (1984) *Flaubert's Parrot*, London: Cape.

Barthes, Roland (1984) *Camera Lucida*, trans. Richard Howard, London: Fontana.

—— (1970) "Historical Discourse," *Structuralism: A Reader*, ed. Michael Lane, London: Cape: 145–55.

—— (1975) *S/Z*, trans. Richard Miller, London: Cape.

—— (1977) "The Death of the Author," in *Image – Music – Text*, trans. Stephen Heath, New York: Hill and Wang, 142–8.

—— (1981) "Theory of the Text," *Untying the Text: A Poststructuralist Reader*, ed. Robert Young, Boston: Routledge: 31–47.

Becker, George J. (ed.) (1963) *Documents of Modern Literary Realism*, Princeton: Princeton University Press.

—— (1963) "Introduction," Becker (ed.), *Documents of Modern Literary Realism*, Princeton: Princeton University Press: 3–38.

—— (1980) *Realism in Modern Literature*, New York: Ungar.

Beckett, Samuel (1977) *Waiting for Godot*, London: Faber and Faber.

Bell, Michael (1983) *The Sentiment of Reality*, London: Allen.

Belsey, Catherine (1980) *Critical Practice*, London: Methuen.

Benamou, Michel (1977) "Presence and Play," in Benamou and Caramello (eds), *Performance in Postmodern Culture*, 3–7.

Benamou, Michel, and Caramello, Charles (eds) (1977) *Performance in Postmodern Culture*, Madison, Wisconsin: Coda.

Benveniste Emile (1977) *Problems in General Linguistics*, trans. Mary Elizabeth Meck, Coral Gables, Florida: University of Miami Press.

Bilan, R. P. (1979) *The Literary Criticism of F.R. Leavis*, Cambridge: Cambridge University Press.

Boyd, John D., S. J. (1968) *The Function of Mimesis and its Decline*, London: Oxford University Press.

Bulwer-Lytton, Edward (1970) "Bulwer-Lytton on Historical Romance," in John O. Hayden (ed). *Scott: The Critical Heritage*, New York, Barnes and Noble, 328–31.

Bush, Douglas (1971) *Matthew Arnold: A Survey of his Poetry and Prose*, London: Macmillan.

Calinescu, Matei (1986) "Postmodernism and Some Paradoxes of Periodization," in Douwe Fokkema and Hans Bertens (eds) *Approaching Postmodernism*; Amsterdam and Philadelphia: John Benjamins, 239–54.

Carlyle, Thomas (1899) "Biography," *Critical and Miscellaneous Essays*, 5 vols, London: Chapman and Hall: 44–61.

—— (1899) "The Death of Goethe," *Critical and Miscellaneous Essays*, 5 vols, London: Chapman and Hall: 374–84.

—— (1899) "On History," *Critical and Miscellaneous Essays*, 5 vols, London: Chapman and Hall: 83–95.

—— (1899) "Sir Walter Scott," *Critical and Miscellaneous Essays*, 5 vols, London: Chapman and Hall: 22–87.

Carpenter, Edmund and McLuhan, Marshall (1960) "Introduction," in Edmund Carpenter and Marshall McLuhan (eds), *Explorations in Communication*, Boston: Beacon Press.

Carroll, David (1982) *The Subject in Question: The Languages of Theory and the Strategies of Fiction*, Chicago: University of Chicago Press.

Cervantes, Miguel de (1950) *Don Quixote*, trans. J. M. Cohen, Harmondsworth: Penguin.

Cockburn, Alexander (1987) "Bus Plunges and Weather Forecasting: Reassurance in the Age of Reagan," American Comparative Literature Association Graduate Student Conference, Cornell University, 10 April.

Cohen, Keith (1979) *Film and Fiction: The Dynamics of Exchange*, New Haven and London: Yale University Press.

Collins, Wilkie (1966) *The Moonstone*, ed. J. I. M. Stewart, Harmondsworth: Penguin.

Courtney, W. L. (1918) *Old Saws and Modern Instances*, Freeport, New York: Books for Libraries Press, 1969.

Cudden, J. A. (1982) *A Dictionary of Literary Terms*, Harmondsworth: Penguin.

Culler, Jonathan (1981) "Literary Competence," in Jane P. Tompkins (ed.), *Reader-Response Criticism: From Formalism to Post-Structuralism*, Baltimore: Johns Hopkins University Press: 101-17.

—— (1982) *On Deconstruction*, Ithaca, New York: Cornell University Press.

Dällenbach, Lucien (1977) *Le récit spéculaire*, Paris: Editions du Seuil.

Derrida, Jacques (1981) *Positions*, trans. Alan Bass, Chicago: University of Chicago Press.

Descartes, René (1968) *Discourse on Method*, trans. F. E. Sutcliffe, Harmondsworth: Penguin.

Desnoyers, Fernand (1963) "On Realism," in George J. Becker (ed.), *Documents of Modern Literary Realism*, Princeton: Princeton University Press: 80-8.

Dyer, Geoff (1985) "Clear Sighted," Review of *Hawksmoor*, by Peter Ackroyd, *New Statesman*, 27 September: 34.

Eagleton, Terry (1983) *Literary Theory*, Minneapolis: University of Minnesota Press.

—— (1985) "Capitalism, Modernism and Postmodernism," *New Left Review*, 152: 60–73.

Eliot, George (1967) *Daniel Deronda*, ed. Barbara Hardy, Harmondsworth: Penguin.

—— (1980) *Adam Bede*, ed. Stephen Gill, Harmondsworth: Penguin.

Ellis, John (1982) *Visible Fictions*, London: Routledge.

Federman, Raymond (ed.) (1975) *Surfiction: Fiction Now and Tomorrow*, Chicago: Swallow Press.

Findley, Timothy (1982) *Famous Last Words*, Toronto: Clarke, Irwin.

Fiske, John and Hartley, John (1978) *Reading Television*, London and New York: Methuen.

Flaubert, Gustave (1983) "On Realism," in George J. Becker (ed.), *Documents of Modern Literary Realism*, Princeton: Princeton University Press: 89–96.

—— (1975) *Madame Bovary*, trans. Alan Russell, Harmondsworth: Penguin.

Fokkema, Douwe and Hans Bertens (eds) (1986) *Approaching Postmodernism*, Amsterdam and Philadelphia: John Benjamins.

Foley, Barbara (1986) *Telling the Truth: The Theory and Practice of Documentary Fiction*, Ithaca, New York: Cornell University Press.

Foucault, Michel (1972) *The Archeology of Knowledge*, trans. A. M. Sheridan Smith, New York: Pantheon.

Fowles, John (1969) *The French Lieutenant's Woman*, Boston and Toronto: Little, Brown and Company.

—— (1974) *Ebony Tower*, Boston and Toronto: Little, Brown and Company.

—— (1977a) *Daniel Martin*, London: Cape.

—— (1977b) *The Magus*, London: Cape.

Freud, Sigmund (1920) *Beyond the Pleasure Principle*, in *The Standard Edition of the Complete Psychological Works of Sigmund Freud*, vol. 18, ed. James Strachey, London: Hogarth Press and The Institute of Psycho-Analysis 1955: 1–64.

Goffman, Erving (1959) *The Presentation of Self in Everyday Life*, Garden City, New York: Doubleday.

Goncourt, Edmond and Jules de. (1963) "Preface," *Germinie Lacerteux*, trans. George J. Becker, in George J. Becker (ed.), *Documents of Modern Literary Realism*, Princeton: Princeton University Press: 117–19.

Graff, Gerald and Reginald Gibbons (eds) (1985) *Criticism in the University*, Evanston, Illinois: Northwestern University Press.

Graff, Gerald (1973) "The Myth of the Postmodernist Breakthrough," *Tri-Quarterly* 26: 383–417.

Gramsci, Antonio (1971) *Selections from The Prison Notebooks of Antonio Gramsci*, eds Quinton Hoare and Geoffrey Nowell Smith, London: Lawrence and Wishart.

Grant, Damian (1970) *Realism*, London: Methuen.

Gray, Alasdair (1981) *Lanark*, Edinburgh: Canongate.

—— (1983) *Unlikely Stories, Mostly*, Edinburgh: Canongate.

—— (1985) *Lanark*, New York: George Braziller Inc.

Greenwood, E. B. (1962) "Reflections on Professor Wellek's Concept of Realism," *Neophilologus* 46: 89–97.

Hardy, Thomas, (1978) *Tess of the D'Urbervilles*, ed. David Skilton, Harmondsworth: Penguin.

Hawkes, Terence, (1977) *Structuralism and Semiotics*, London: Methuen.

Haycraft, Howard, (1941) *Murder for Pleasure: The Life and Times of the Detective Story*, New York: Appleton-Century.

Hayden, John O. (ed.) (1970) *Scott: The Critical Heritage*, New York: Barnes and Noble.

Hazlitt, William (1969) *The Spirit of the Age or Contemporary Portraits*, ed. E. D. Hackerness, London and Glasgow: Collins.

Heller, Erich, (1963) "The Realistic Fallacy," in George J. Becker (ed.), *Documents of Modern Literary Realism*, Princeton: Princeton University Press: 591–8.

Hemmings, F. W. J., (ed.) (1974) *The Age of Realism*, Harmondsworth: Penguin.

Hollinghurst, Alan (1985) "In Hieroglyph and Shadow," Review of *Hawksmoor*, by Peter Ackroyd, *Times Literary Supplement*, 27 September: 1049.

Holquist, Michael (1971) "Whodunit and Other Questions: Meta-physical Detective Stories in Post-War Fiction," *New Literary History* 3 no. 1: 135–56.

Hughes, Robert (1980) *The Shock of the New*, New York: Knopf.

Hutcheon, Linda (1980) *Narcissistic Narrative: The Metafictional Paradox*, New York and London: Methuen, 1984.

―― (1987) "Beginning to Theorize Postmodernism," *Textual Practice* 1: 10–31.

―― (1988) *A Poetics of Postmodernism: History, Theory, Fiction*, New York and London: Routledge.

Iser, Wolfgang (1974) *The Implied Reader*, Baltimore and London: Johns Hopkins University Press.

James, Henry (1864) "Fiction and Sir Walter Scott," Review of *Essays on Fiction*, by Nassau W. Senior, *North American Review*, October; xcix: 580–7.

―― (1957) "The Art of Fiction," *The House of Fiction*, ed. Leon Edel, Westport, Connecticut: Greenwood, 1973: 23–45.

―― (1962) *The Art of the Novel*, New York: Scribner's.

―― (1974) *The Portrait of a Lady*, Harmondsworth: Penguin.

Jameson, Frederic (1972) *The Prison-House of Language: A Critical Account of Structuralism and Russian Formalism*, Princeton and London: Princeton University Press.

―― (1984) "Postmodernism, or the Cultural Logic of Late Capitalism," *New Left Review* 146: 53–92.

―― (1985) "Postmodernism and Consumer Society," Hal Foster (ed.), *Postmodern Culture*, London and Sydney: Pluto Press: 111–25.

Johnston, Kelvin (1983) Review of *Chekhov's Journey*, by Ian Watson, *Observer*, 20 February: 33.

Kaminsky, Alice R. (1974) "On Literary Realism," in John Halperin (ed.), *The Theory of the Novel*, London: Oxford University Press: 213–32.

Keates, Jonathan (1985) "Creaking Floorboards," Review of *Hawksmoor*, by Peter Ackroyd, *Observer*, 22 September: 27.

King, Stephen (1987) *Misery*, New York: Viking/Penguin.

Kutnick, Jerzy (1986) *The Novel as Performance: The Fiction of Ronald Sukenick and Raymond Federman*, Carbondale, Illinois: Southern Illinois University Press.

Lawrence, D. H. (1950) *The White Peacock*, Harmondsworth: Penguin.

Leavis, F. R. (1933) *For Continuity*, Cambridge: Minority Press.

―― (1934) "Literary Criticism and Philosophy," *Scrutiny* 5, 59–70.

―― (1969) *The Common Pursuit*, Harmondsworth: Penguin.

―― (1970) *D. H. Lawrence: Novelist*, Harmondsworth: Penguin.

―― (1972) *The Great Tradition*, Harmondsworth: Penguin.

―― and Denys Thompson (1933) *Culture and Environment*, London: Chatto and Windus, 1964.

Levine, George (1974) "Realism Reconsidered," in John Halperin (ed.), *The Theory of the Novel*, London: Oxford University Press: 233–6.

―― (1981) *The Realistic Imagination*, Chicago: Chicago University Press.

Lodge, David, (1983) *The British Museum is Falling Down*, Harmondsworth: Penguin.
Lyotard, Jean-François (1984) *The Postmodern Condition: A Report on Knowledge*, trans. Geoff Bennington and Brian Massumi, Minneapolis: University of Minnesota Press.
McHale, Brian (1987) *Postmodernist Fiction*, New York and London: Methuen.
de Man, Paul (1986) *The Resistance to Theory*, Minneapolis: University of Minnesota Press.
Michaels, W. B., and Knapp, Stephen (1982) "Against Theory," *Critical Inquiry* 8: 723–42.
Miller, J. Hillis (1974) "Narrative and History," *English Literary History* 41: 455–73.
Moretti, Franco (1983) *Signs Taken for Wonders*, trans. Susan Fischer *et al.*, London: Verso.
Newman, Charles (1985) *The Post-Modern Aura: The Act of Fiction in an Age of Inflation*, Evanston, Illinois: Northwestern University Press.
Nochlin, Linda (1976) *Realism*, Harmondsworth: Penguin.
Norris, Christopher (1982) *Deconstruction: Theory and Practice*, London: Methuen.
Olshen, Barry (1978) *John Fowles*, New York: Ungar.
Owens, Craig (1985) "The Discourse of Others: Feminists and Postmodernism," in Hal Foster (ed.), *Postmodern Culture*, London and Sydney: Pluto Press, 57–82.
Palmer, Richard (1977) "Toward a Postmodern Hermeneutics of Performance," in Michel Benamou and Charles Caramello (eds), *Performance in Postmodern Culture*, Madison, Wisconsin: Coda: 19–32.
Parrinder, Patrick (1977) *Authors and Authority: A Study of English Literary Criticism and its Relation to Culture 1750–1900*, London and Boston: Routledge.
Passmore, John (1968) *A Hundred Years of Philosophy*, Harmondsworth: Penguin.
Plato (1967) *The Republic. Literary Criticism: Plato to Dryden*, trans. and ed. Allan H. Gilbert, Detroit: Wayne State University Press.
Prince, Gerald (1980) "Notes on the Text as Reader," in Susan R. Suleiman and Inge Crosman (eds), *The Reader in the Text*, Princeton: Princeton University Press: 225–40.
Robinson, Heather (1987) "New Recruits in the War for Ratings," *Maclean's* 100 no. 40, 5 October: 69–70.
Rushdie, Salman (1981) *Midnight's Children*, London: Picador.
Ruskin, John (1903–12a) *Modern Painters*, vols. 3–7 of *The Works of Ruskin*, eds E. T. Cook and Alexander Wedderburn, 39 vols, London: George Allan.
—— (1903–12b) "The Queen of the Air," *The Works of John Ruskin*, eds E. T. Cook and Alexander Wedderburn, 39 vols, London: George Allan: 283–423.
Said, Edward (1983) *The World, the Text, and the Critic*, Cambridge,

Mass.: Harvard University Press.

Saussure, Ferdinand de (1915) *Course in General Linguistics*, trans. Wade Baskin, eds Charles Balley, Albert Sechehaye, and Albert Reidlinger, London: Peter Owen, 1974.

Schrank, Jeffrey (1977) *Snap, Crackle, and Popular Taste: The Illusion of Free Choice in America*, New York: Delacorte Press.

Schechner, Richard (1983) "News, Sex, and Performance Theory," Ihab Hassan and Sally Hassan (eds), *Innovation/Renovation: New Perspectives on the Humanities*, Madison, Wisconsin: University of Wisconsin Press: 189–224.

Scott, Walter (1818) *The Heart of Midlothian*, 2 vols, Boston: Estes and Lauriat, 1893.

—— (1819) *Ivanhoe*, 2 vols, Boston: Estes and Lauriat, 1893.

—— (1823) *Peveril of the Peak*, 3 vols, Boston: Estes and Lauriat, 1893.

Silverman, Kaja (1983) *The Subject of Semiotics*, New York: Oxford University Press.

Spanos, William V. (1972) "The Detective and the Boundary: Some Notes on the Postmodern Literary Imagination," *Boundary* 2 no. 1: 147–68.

Stang, Richard (1961) *The Theory of the Novel in England 1850–1870*, New York: Columbia University Press.

Stendhal (1830) *Scarlet and Black: A Chronicle of the Nineteenth Century*, trans. Margaret R. B. Shaw, Harmondsworth: Penguin, 1953.

Stephen, Leslie (1874–9) *Hours in a Library*, 4 vols, New York: Knickerbocker Press, n.d.

Stern, J. P. (1973) *On Realism*, London: Routledge.

Sterne, Laurence (1967) *The Life and Opinions of Tristram Shandy*, ed. Graham Petrie, Harmondsworth: Penguin.

Swift, Graham (1983) *Waterland*, London: Heinemann.

Sukenick, Ronald (1985) *In Form: Digressions on the Art of Fiction*, Carbondale and Edwardsville: Southern Illinois University Press.

Suleiman, Susan (1980) "Introduction: Varieties of Audience-Oriented Criticism," in Susan Suleiman and Inge Crosman (eds), *The Reader in the Text: Essays on Audience and Interpretation*, New Jersey: Princeton University Press.

Symons, Julian (1985) *Bloody Murder*, Harmondsworth: Penguin.

Thackeray, William (1978) *Vanity Fair*, ed. J. I. M. Stewart, Harmondsworth: Penguin.

Thomas, D. M. (1981) *The White Hotel*, Harmondsworth: Penguin.

Timeline World History Chart (1987) Advertizement in *The Atlantic* 260, September: 37.

Todorov, Tzvetan (1975) *The Fantastic: A Structural Approach to a Literary Genre*, trans. Richard Howard, Ithaca, New York: Cornell University Press.

—— (1977) *The Poetics of Prose*, trans. Richard Howard, Ithaca, New York: Cornell University Press.

Tompkins, Jane P. (1981) "An Introduction to Reader-Response

Criticism," in Jane P. Tompkins (ed.), *Reader-Response Criticism: From Formalism to Post-Structuralism*, Baltimore: Johns Hopkins University Press: ix-xxvi.

Watson, Ian (1983) *Chekhov's Journey*, London: Gollancz.

Watt, Ian (1957) *The Rise of the Novel: Studies in Defoe, Richardson and Fielding*, Harmondsworth: Penguin.

Waugh, Patricia (1984) *Metafiction: The Theory and Practice of Self-Conscious Fiction*, London and New York: Methuen.

—— (1989) *Feminine Fictions: Revisiting the Postmodern*, New York and London: Routledge.

Wellek, René (1961) "The Concept of Realism in Literary Scholarship," *Neophilologus* 45: 1–20.

—— (1962) "A Reply to E.B. Greenwood's Reflections," *Neophilologus* 46: 194–6.

—— (1966) *The Later Nineteenth Century*, vol. 4 of *A History of Modern Criticism 1750–1950*, 5 vols, New Haven: Yale University Press.

White, Hayden (1973) *Metahistory: The Historical Imagination in Nineteenth-Century Europe*, Baltimore: Johns Hopkins University Press.

—— (1976) "The Fictions of Factual Representation," in Angus Fletcher (ed.), *The Literature of Fact*, New York: Columbia University Press: 21–44.

—— (1978) "The Historical Text as Literary Artifact," Robert H. Canary and Henry Kozicki (eds), *The Writing of History: Literary Form and Historical Understanding*, Madison, Wisconsin: University of Wisconsin Press: 41–62.

Williams, Ioan (1975) *The Realist Novel in England*, Pittsburgh: University of Pittsburgh Press.

Williams, Nigel (1985) *Star Turn*, London: Faber.

Williams, Raymond (1976) *Keywords*, Glasgow: Collins.

Williamson, Judith (1985) *Consuming Passions: The Dynamics of Popular Culture*, London and New York: Marion Boyars.

Wimsatt, W. K. and Beardsley, Monroe C. (1954a) "The Affective Fallacy," in *The Verbal Icon*, Kentucky: University Press of Kentucky: 21–39.

—— (1954b) "The Intentional Fallacy," in *The Verbal Icon*, Kentucky: University Press of Kentucky: 3–18.

Zola, Emile (1867) *Thérèse Raquin*, trans. Leonard Tancock, Harmondsworth: Penguin, 1984.

—— (1963) "The Experimental Novel," in George J. Becker (ed.), *Documents of Modern Literary Realism*, Princeton: Princeton University Press: 162–96.

Index